The Heart of Cozy

A collection of reflections that inspire cozy living
and nurture a heart of faith.

MONICA WILKINSON

THE HEART OF COZY
A collection of reflections that inspire cozy living
and nurture a heart of faith.

All photos in this book were taking by the author with the exception of the following:
Cover photo, back cover author photo and photo on pages iv, 25, 279
and 280 taken by Emily Wilkinson.
Photo on page 172 taken by Rachel Wilkinson.
Author photo on page 282 taken by Becky Kyle, Good Photo Colorado Springs, CO.
Photo on page 276 taken by Jessica Clayton at Camp Cozy.
Photo on page 247 taken by Jen Lints, jenlintsphotography.com.

ISBN-13: 979-8-218-04368-1

Emily, Carolyn, Leandra, Shay and Tanya – your kind and genuine friendship and accountability are a gift to me. I love each of you and am so grateful you are in my life.

Rachel for the encouragement and inspiration to press on with this collection of "cozy-isms" – I love you.

Introduction

As I write this, I'm snuggled up in a dim corner of our living room in my thrifted yellow quiet time chair. I'm ensconced in slippers, cozy socks, a scarf, and a wrap and I have a soft knitted blanket tossed over my lap. To say that I have all my cozy on is an understatement. Nearby, two of our three teenagers are singing, chatting, and playing a game while our living room is definitely rocking the lived-in look!

If our family had a favorite word, it would probably be *cozy*. We love all the cozy things, and even our dog appreciates this luxury when he burrows under flannel sheets to get warm on a cold night. Ha!

I've spent the past couple of years learning that I love to write cozy words, words that create a sense of warmth and comfort but also bring us together through common everyday happenings that we see and experience. While there seems to be an abundance of books available on cozy living, I haven't seen many that wrap the whole heart of the believer into this cozy lifestyle.

It is important to recognize and remind each other that the true meaning of cozy does not ignore sorrow, hardship, or suffering. Cozy does not mean that life is always soft and comfy and a perfectly manicured bed of roses. Here is where the spiritual parallel begins – cozy gives us a soft place to land (thank you Candace for this phrase!) during these trials of life and allows us opportunity to give comfort to those around us who are hurting. Through this serving and receiving of comfort, we learn more about the heart of our heavenly Father. He does not value our comfort above all else, no – He values holiness and obedience. Yet He is a place of refuge, a comfort to us. He is our soft place to land, and this is what we want to model for those around us – especially to a watching world who needs Him desperately.

Through writing cozy poems, reflections, and articles, I've regretted only one thing: that in writing for secular publications, I can't openly weave the heart of faith into articles that value the warmth of candles and the familiar joy of home. This book was born out of a desire to continue to write about things that evoke a sense of cozy but also envelop the heart of the believer.

My hope is that in the midst of the uncertainty all around us, this book will be a warm hug, a kind friend, and will bring a nod of understanding as you see yourself in the joy of putting on jammies, cutting wildflowers, or ladling a bowl of soup on a cold evening.

This is a sensory book about the simple pleasures we can enjoy on ordinary days. It is also a call to long for our heavenly home, which will take these dim feelings of cozy and bring us into full delight in the Lord's presence.

In these pages, I have written about things that feel cozy to me, like the experience of home being a sweet gift, and memories that invoke a sense of belonging. I humbly realize that you may not have had the same experiences, or that the things I write may be different than what you find cozy. And I genuinely pray that this is not offensive or hurtful to you in any way. What I am trying to do is invite you in to this world of cozy living, of embracing simple, ordinary things that show us more of the Lord and welcomes us into what true coziness is: the warmth of being wanted by our heavenly Father, the joy of delighting in all of His gifts, and the sweet comfort of sharing His love with those around us (even as we learn to accept it ourselves).

If you have picked up this book and not yet met my friend Jesus, I would be honored to introduce you to Him. I've written a special note just for you on page 271.

For now, the door is open wide and a candle is lit, so please take off your shoes and make yourself at home. I am extending a warm welcome to you, dear reader, and inviting you in to the Heart of Cozy.

Snuggled up and grateful you are here –

Monica

Table of Contents

Gifts of Nature

Beauty of Apples 15
Campfires 19
Golden Hour 23
Rosy Cheeks 27
Light 31
Hidden Work 35
After a Hard Day 39
Sun through the Window 43
Daffodils 45
A Walk in the Woods 49
Quaking Aspens 53
Camp Cozy 57
Blueberries 61
Nature Goodies 65
Queen Anne's Lace 71
Boat Landing 75

Invitations to Imagine

Story and Sip..79
Kingdom Outpost..83
Weathered Barns 87
Glow from the Windows..91

Refuge on Wheels 95
Cute Roads 99
Heavenly Homeland 101
Farmhouse 105
Sparkles of Light 109

The Refuge and Realness of Home

Fading Light 115
The Yellow Apartment 119
Jammies 123
A Candle on the Porch 127
Gray Days 131
Patchwork Quilt 133
The Attic 137
The Glorious Smallness of Home 141
Warm Apple Butter 145
Weight of Blankets 151
A Warm Welcome 155
An Ordinary Evening at Home 159
Yellow Chair 161

The Imperfect Beauty and Shelter of Relationships

Frayed Edges 167
Miss Sue's Popcorn 169
Porch Swing 173
The Mommy Touch 177
Let's Talk about Our Day 181
Tables 183

Creating an Inviting Atmosphere 187
Summer Evening 189
Missing Dad's Voice 193
The Comfy Test 195
Strawberry Picking 197
Childhood Sick Days 201
Fun Team 205
Picnics 207

Everyday Magic of Simple Pleasures

Enamelware 213
The Ministry of Soup 215
Warm Laundry 221
A Fluffy Scarf 223
Waiting for the Lids to Pop 225
Smiling about Thermoses 229
Free Fruit 233
Noticing Small 237
Toast and Tea 241
Seasonal Joys 245
Soup and Grilled Cheese 253
Homemade Ice Cream 257
Bread 261

A Special Invitation

"Well, Come In!" 271

Gifts of Nature

Beauty of Apples

Stepping out of the car, we are instantly welcomed with the sweet and spicy aroma of cider, fresh donuts, and fallen apples languishing on the ground. Eager anticipation flows through our minds as we approach the stacks of weathered bushel baskets waiting to be filled with red, gold, and green jewels hanging on the trees in abundance.

Walking into the orchard with empty baskets swinging at our sides, the day is full of promise and excitement. We scan the rows for the varieties that welcome us like old friends or that call to us with the possibility of trying something new. Gala, Granny Smith, Jonagold, Asian Pear, Honeycrisp, and Golden Delicious – their names are familiar, and we appreciate each one for the benefits they boast. Mouths start to water as we imagine the taste of a crisp apple straight from the tree, and we can list a host of recipes we want to enjoy with this basket of treasured fruit.

Imagination takes flight as we stand beside heavily laden trees, looking for just the right apples to choose. Light filters through leaves, the sky peeks through, and there is beauty hanging on branches all around. Picking one with a leaf or two attached adds to the charm, and we take a picture in our mind's eye and maybe even with our cameras. Gently laying each sphere of fruit into the basket, we add layer upon layer until they are heaped up to the top. Can we fit another one in? This beautiful one we just can't pass by?

Walking back toward the car is not quite as simple as when our baskets were empty. We are heavily laden now and the sun has inched higher in the sky. The smells in the air cause a rumble in our tummies and a little watering in our mouth for the delicious taste of a juicy, crisp apple. Or perhaps sipping a cider slushy and stopping by the window where a chalkboard boasts fresh apple cider donuts. We follow our nose toward this heavenly scent. Warm rings of fried dough dusted in cinnamon and sugar are ready and waiting for our enjoyment!

A picnic basket is brought from the car, and alongside the edge of the orchard, we find a table. Laying out a cloth and simple fare from home, we pull out fresh apples and prove once again that food eaten outside is a delight to our senses.

As we head home, the smells, tastes, and sights of apples create a layer of memories that we carry with us into the days ahead. We will be back next year, and this visit will fill our hearts and minds until then.

Campfires

A song from my growing-up years starts out …

> *"It only takes a spark to get a fire going,*
> *and soon all those around can warm up in its glowing…"*

The sparks begin to sizzle and pop, the scent of woodsy smoke hovers nearby, and as flames begin to flicker, so my mind flickers and echoes through the corridors of time with the memories of campfires over the years.

Camping as a little girl and getting my blue tennis shoes so close to the fires that they scorched. A fun Halloween night with three littles of my own as we roasted hotdogs and made popcorn and s'mores over the fire. The time my dad heated rocks in the fire to wrap and put at our feet because it was so cold while we were camping and the times it has been too wet to have a fire because of rain.

I hear giggles and laughter, remember bowls of popcorn and stories created from nonsensical Mad Libs. I remember the time I had a handful of friends over and we sat in our yard around the fire wrapped in quilts, expressing gratitude for the strengths and blessings visible in each person present. A smile comes to my face as I recall the cans of Van Camp's Pork & Beans cooked right on the fire with the lid cocked open and steaming hot. Dad would pick it up with tongs and serve it with our campy dinner. It has brought joy to sit around the fire with my own family now, making memories together as we play the movie game, where you give clues until the others can guess which movie you are thinking of. It's simple, maybe, but we laugh and get silly, and those are the heady things of treasured memories.

There is the anticipation of being all warm and snuggly in a sleeping bag on a camping trip, only to hear someone already outside, rustling to get a fire going. Pretty soon, the sounds of pop and crackle are compelling enough to make a dash for it from one warm spot to another.

There is the gathering of twigs and sticks for kindling and the trademark scent that lingers on my husband's flannel shirt or on the edges of hair swishing around my shoulders. Stirring the embers with a stick sends up a mini firework display of sparks that lights the night and creates a gasp of wonder. It only takes a spark to ignite my memory into a blazing warmth that lingers past the last glow of the dying embers.

Golden Hour

The sky begins to glow.

The edges tinge with pink.

It looks as though an artist has picked up a brush, dipped the bristles in shades of yellow, hues of orange, and whispers of pink, and is making sweeping strokes across the sky.

Cotton candy puffs of clouds are piled up in blushes and blues.

Each time the golden hour arrives, it enchants, and each painting is different than the others. This one is new and has never been experienced before.

The rising sun adds golden highlights and honeyed hues to everything it touches. Sparkles of sunlight dance on the water, filter gently through trees, and stream into my dining room, casting a glow that catches my eye and makes me realize something is different about the light.

Each moment, the sky and light change into something seemingly more beautiful than the moment before. Colors deepen and grow richer, the sky is a canvas for the most stunning artwork to be created right before our eyes in a new and fresh way each time. It has familiar notes and hues, but the masterpiece is unique each time.

This time of day is so special. It is worth letting my feet carry me outside, lifting my eyes upward to feel it touch my face. A deep breath gives me a moment of pause and peace.

Pictures taken at this time of day attempt to capture some of the warmth, and they do, but they also don't. It is something that needs to be experienced in person. To watch the world turn varying shades of warm and inviting colors that soften the harsh edges of the day and settle my heart in a way that catches my breath with its beauty.

Rosy Cheeks

Nip in the air
Nips my nose
Sets my teeth to chatter

Seeing my breath
Tingly cheeks
Hands in cozy mittens

Bounce in my step
Frost on the trees
All of nature sparkles

When I get home
And start to thaw
A happy glow settles in

Mug of hot cocoa
Hands wrapped around
Feeling the warmth trickle down

Cheeks start to thaw
Slippers warm feet
Quilt cuddled over my lap

That rosy-cheek feeling
Makes me smile
It puts a spring in my step

It lights up my eyes
Gets my blood moving
Warms me from the inside out

Lights up my soul
Inspires my thoughts
Cultivates good ideas

All it takes
Is a walk in the cold
Coming home with rosy cheeks

They feel tight and tingly
They make me feel cheerful
I just want them to stay that way

Perhaps it's because
Cold days are rare
We want to soak it all in

Rosy cheeks
Small and sweet little gift
Grateful to be alive

Light

Advent is approaching, and the thought of light is filling my mind. I'm excited to host some ladies from our church for an Advent study over four Wednesdays in December. In an adventurous decision, it will be held at our small town's waterfront park.

A basket of blankets and quilts will be toted to set underneath a wooden table in case we get chilly. Candles will crowd the weathered tabletop as darkness will hang heavy over the space where guests will be welcomed. Vintage plaid thermoses will wait on the stone ledge with spiced cider to delight tongues and warm hands.

My prayer is that this will be a pause and opportunity to slow and savor the holiness of the season. To see how bright the light is when the dark seems complete and enveloping. We know that Jesus is the Light of the World, and what better way to bring this to life than to sit in a public park with lights dancing among us?

Not only among us, but His light dances within us and hopefully pours out of us into a watching world in need of light. Light is warm and inviting; it can be mesmerizing and can draw us close. Light says someone is here and cared enough to create a warm glow to say – we're home, we're waiting for you, you are welcome! Arriving home or being invited to a home filled with light fills more than just our eyes. It warms hearts and minds, it warms our sense of belonging and being wanted.

No one wants us more than Jesus, the Light of the World. His is the softest yet brightest, purest and most complete light. It is the warmest light known as, in fact, He is the creator of light.

Twinkling Christmas lights catch our eye, candlelight makes our eyes sparkle and evokes a sense of magic and mystery, and firelight beckons with warmth, scent, and crackling sparks. Porch lights welcome us to the door of a friend, and we see light in the eyes and hear light in voices. Light can fill our hearts when we look to the right kinds of light and to the one true source of light.

Darkness actually accentuates the light even more. One little speck is suddenly visible where in daylight it has gone unnoticed and hidden. The light of Christ fills our hearts and pours over, under, around, and through us. Our homes are like lighthouses shining a beacon of light that offers safe harbor and haven to those bobbing in the water, needing a life ring of hope.

That hope is more than a shot in the dark – it is sun whispers streaming through the clouds, giving us a glimpse of heaven, embers of another day fading in the glow of the sky as the earth rotates away from the sun, reflections through windows and mirrors that multiply light. Our hope is sure when we have placed it in the Light of the World – Jesus Himself.

He is our light, and we are light-bearers to the darkness that seems to surround us. Lord, may Your light shine brightly through us to bring the warmth of hope and Your inviting presence to a dark and cold world.

glorify
THERMOS

Hidden Work

Winter invites times of stillness, of darkness lengthening, of nature quieting. It is the time of year when we are giddy about choosing a new calendar and seeing all of those white spaces – open squares with no commitments to fill them yet. Nature models white space for us, as well: the layers of greens have changed into reds, yellows, oranges, and finally browns as the leaves fall and crunch underfoot. The bare branches allow lots of margin in our view, and snow only adds to the literal white space of the view out the window.

One February, I purposed to spend five minutes a day being still. Five minutes is just enough to admit that I can't make excuses about not having enough time, but I found that often, those five minutes turned into more minutes. Minutes spent reading, sitting still, watching my kids play, watching the sky, or praying. Imagine the cumulative effort if we would spend only five minutes a day being still. Over the course of one year, that would add up to over thirty hours spent in stillness. Now imagine the implications to your body and soul those minutes of stillness would bring. Once we start recognizing the beauty of stillness, we may find ourselves beginning to look for ways to find more of it and to incorporate it into our daily lives and rhythms.

There is a phrase that has made its way into my heart and mind frequently over the past couple of years: hidden work. As winter nears, it seems the right time to pause and consider its meaning. Nature pulls in to the quiet hush of a slower season, and we don't see signs of life from many of the plants around us. The hidden work takes place beneath the surface, in the dark and quiet places. One of the mysteries of plants and trees around us is how many of them have a dormant season.

Many varieties of trees and plants are barren and sparse all winter. But under the surface, in the quiet shadows, work is still taking place. Roots are still alive; energy is being restored and stored up for the coming seasons of growth, production, and harvest. Taking our cues from nature, winter is a season that can promote stillness and rest for us, as well. Work takes place under the surface in the hidden places – but that work mainly involves being still and taking a long break from producing and bearing fruit and blooming.

Living in the Deep South, I've seen firsthand how plants struggle without the rest of winter. When temperatures don't get cold enough, these plants just grow and grow year-round, and eventually they grow themselves to death. They've had no rest, no healing time, no time for the hidden work.

In the same way, we cannot expect to always be in seasons of growth, blooming, and producing a fruitful harvest. We, too, can grow ourselves to death – at least in figurative terms. Our bodies and souls need time to recharge and focus on this hidden work for the next season of growth and production that will come our way.

Looking at many calendars, our winters don't follow this example of purposeful white space, and we wonder why we are burned out, exhausted and depleted by the time we turn a leaf on a new year. A new calendar page waits with blank squares – open and white and clean. Unhurried and unrushed. These white spaces give us room to breathe, to be, to rest, and to grow in hidden ways that will strengthen our inner roots. Shallow roots are weak and easily destroyed, but deep roots have beautiful strength for storms on the horizon.

Photographers and designers will tell you that rooms and images need white space, a place for your eyes to land. Consider this white space – this hidden and quiet work – a place for your soul to land: to dream, to explore creativity, to listen, to slow, and to invest in your inner self.

To create these open spaces may mean saying no to some things so that you are able to say yes to what your soul needs more. A white space means just that – *space*. Space to be still, to pause, and to recover from other busy seasons.

Fear of missing out may give you reason to pause and consider if white space and stillness are worth it, but you will miss so much more if you refuse it. Give yourself the gift of a few minutes of stillness a day, and keep an eye on those white spaces – you are the boss of your calendar. You tell it what to do. It is your servant, not your master.

White space on the calendar, white space in nature, and white space in your soul. These spaces make room for the hidden work and winter is the perfect time to enjoy and cultivate these hidden work moments that can nourish the inner roots of our spirit. We will find that they will refresh and rejuvenate us for future seasons of growth and bounty.

Winter brings a natural pause, a glow from windows inviting us into the warmth of home, a crisp rosy-cheek feeling as the air turns icy, and a reminder to pause and let our roots be nourished through rest.

After a Hard Day

Some days are just plain hard, no matter how much we may try to avoid it. And more than that, some seasons are so hard we aren't sure we can make it through.

Our family walked through a very long, difficult season with my dad's illness – an entire decade. And as that season came to a close and we said goodbye to him, the days were draining, exhausting, and full of all the feelings, with a myriad of details to manage in a short time and near Christmas.

One afternoon, I was so weary and depleted. My mom was continuing to make calls and tend to things that I couldn't do for her, so I grabbed my three kids and dog and headed for a nearby park - a place we have gone over the years to admire the view, climb the red and white marbled rocks, and marvel over the wildflowers, pinecones, and weeds made art by the light shining through them. My camera was our only other companion, and we had a mere hour before dusk began to settle, but that one hour was a gift of beauty.

Beauty is a balm to the weary soul because the beautiful things we experience each and every day are a glorious creation of God, and this creation was made to worship and glorify Him! So when we are enjoying it, we are in a sanctuary of praise, surrounded by worship that lifts our eyes and hearts to remember who He is.

As we hiked up dirt paths and gasped over golden hour light spilling between pine boughs and sparkling through wheat-colored tendrils, my soul breathed a deep exhale. I was filled up, and this small pause was the boost I needed to return and face the hard things awaiting. The warmth of that hour filled me with remembrance of God's goodness, hope, and peace, breathing in the possibility that I would feel again and I would continue to enjoy His creation and His beauty.

Crunchy leaves on bare branches. Little hidden patches of snow in the shadows. My children smiling. Our dog sniffing. Snapping a few photos is not life-changing, but it can be perspective-lifting. Pausing to place one foot in front of the other and breathe the fresh air is a reminder that this is a day He has made and given, all for His glory and out of His love.

Creation does what it was made to do.

It keeps on going until He says differently. Even when we are facing grief, pastel colors will still tinge the edges of the horizon at sunset, and the woodsy scent of spicy pines will still provide a comforting aroma to those who walk among the boughs. May we always be curious at what lies around the next bend, for it will always, always continue to point to our dear heavenly Father.

Sun through the Window

On a regular Monday afternoon, I sit on the couch to fold laundry. It is a chilly day, and the sun streams through the blinds onto the edges of the couch. I find myself leaning toward the sun to feel the warmth through the window – to feel the golden hues warm my body and soul. As the sun moves, so do I, trying to stay in the beam's warm embrace.

It is funny to me that at certain times of the year, I avoid the sun because I'm tired of being hot. But then when the air outside cools down, the sun magically becomes a delight as I desire to sit and bask in its warm glow. There is something restorative to it, and I feel it sink deep into my bones.

When I sit in the presence of Jesus, God's Son, it has a similar effect. It draws me to a deeper appreciation of who He is and a deeper understanding of His character. It stirs my heart to respond, and I want to do whatever it takes to stay in His presence. I want to feel His favor and love pouring out warmth and life to my heart, just as the sun rays pour through our living room window.

Daffodils

As little green shoots begin to peek their heads through the soil, spring begins to emerge into view. Early spring brings the joys of watching the saucer magnolia trees around our neighborhood with their tall pods of pink waiting to open into large, beautiful blooms. We are always surprised by them, as it seems Christmas is barely over and the buds are standing at the ready to open up to the promise of newness.

A few weeks later, we watch the posts on Facebook to see when it will be time to make our annual jaunt to a local farm providing you-pick daffodils. It's nothing fancy – a big open field with rows upon rows of daffodils. They don't all bloom at once, and they vary in color – white, yellow, and the two combined. The heady floral scent still fills my mind eleven months later as I'm eagerly awaiting another opportunity to pick up a plastic sand pail and pair of scissors and point my rubber boots out to the rows of dancing beauties waiting to charm our table.

Some ladies bring baskets and drape the handles over their arms, and I know immediately they are kindred spirits. I wish I had thought to bring a basket, too! We will cut extras and make sure we have blooms to gather into small bouquets and share, always happy for a way to delight others.

As with other things, the daffodil fields remind me of days when my children were young, like the days when our second daughter had an American Girl Bitty Baby strapped in a baby carrier on her back, rubber boots on her feet, and a fuzzy hat that covered her ears, all while cutting the little green stems and collecting beauty in her own wonderful, special way.

It reminds me of the time my sister was in the hospital awaiting the arrival of her youngest baby, and I was praying for their safety and comfort while a vase of daffodils adorned my table. It's amazing how memories that contain just a simple everyday item can become emblazoned in our hearts and minds when the circumstances surrounding that item heightened our senses.

Spring is a reminder that God renews the earth and sustains it through certain rhythms that we can count on year after year. Some years, we may have fewer daffodils to choose from – but spring will always come. He is so good to provide beauty through nature to lace our days and our memories.

A Walk in the Woods

Leaves crunch under my feet while canopies of branches arch overhead. The moist moss, decomposing leaves and spicy wood scent the air and arrest my senses. Stepping into the woods, I feel the world slow down, and both the temperature and pace drop in the shadows. Sunlight breaks through every now and then and creates a variegated tapestry of rich browns and greens.

It seems to me that one reason nature is so refreshing and calming is that it is created by God to praise Him. In this sense, when I am outdoors, I am in a sanctuary of praise where all of creation cries out in glory and praise to God, for that is what He made it to do!

As I walk in the woods, sit by a stream, or hike through the hills, my mind fills with wonder at each tiny detail. A scalloped little fungus clinging to the trunk of a tree, a miniature pinecone, feathers from a bird, various blooms and pods, a leaf that catches my eye. When we stop to really look, we will see amazing things in a drop of water, the way a tree fell and has now become part of the forest in its fallen state, or a little bend in the path lined with wildflowers.

The trickle of water may greet our ears as it dances over and around rocks, twigs, and logs. Light sparkles with each little movement of the stream, and it smooths not only the rough edges of rocks but also the rough edges in my heart that need to pause and be still.

Woodsy fresh air fills my lungs and clears the cobwebs from my mind. It is such a delightful way to create a change of scenery and pace, refresh my perspective, remember how small I am, and be re-inspired in creativity.

Perhaps you prefer the beach or a quiet lakeside. Maybe a park near your home or even your front porch – it is amazing what marvels of nature we can observe without even leaving home if we are still and quiet enough to let ourselves discover them. Just sitting on my front porch, I watch the sky and how the clouds move. I see a butterfly visit each flower in our yard, and I sit very still so the hummingbird won't be afraid to approach the feeder overhead. A bird perches on our mailbox or in the neighbors' ornamental pear tree, and I smile at his boldness to sing so loud and clear.

The point is this: God's creation is restoring to us, and one reason He made it is for our enjoyment! What a delight to be outside amongst the symphony of praise crying out to Him every day. No wonder it restores my spirit to take a walk in the woods.

Quaking Aspens

Up in the mountains
Grows the aspen tree
Standing straight and tall
For all of us to see

White and nubby bark
Not too big around
A network of roots
Connected underground

Winter bare and plain
Blending in to snow
Crisp blue sky and sun
Each casting a shadow

Spring begins to thaw
Buds begin to form
Tiny leaves appear
Holding tight through a storm

Summer brings green leaves
Circular and small
Breeze begins to blow
Quaking their trademark call

Fall lights up the hills
With each golden hue
Sunlight streaming down
A stunning autumn view

Going on a walk
Picking up some leaves
Pressing in a book
Creating memories

Gentle quaking leaves
Smooth and strong and green
Feeling like I'm home
Wherever they are seen

Slow and quiet sound
Sitting on a hill
Grove of quaking leaves
Inviting me to still

Just a humble tree
Beautiful all year
Drawing me to quiet
Delightful sound to hear

c a m
c o z y

Camp Cozy

Nestled in the foothills of the North Carolina mountains is a neighborhood we love to visit. The windy road leading up to it is lined with trees, wildflowers, and a mountain creek here and there. We pass cabins, homey looking gardens, and single lane bridges. Pulling in through the gate, we head straight for the campground. A steep gravel road leads down to the lush green of trees and moss, and we drive through the creek to get over to the side where campsites and picnic tables await.

Tiny orange mushrooms are like sprinkles amongst the grass. A swing is perched on the hill of one bank, inviting guests to come and sit a spell and admire the view and the stillness. Children run for red buckets intended to help put out fires and instead catch craw-dads in the creek or build cairns and little rafts made from nature items.

Two blue Adirondack chairs have aged and weathered almost to the point of ruin, and a split rail fence divides the road from our campsite. Pulling in, we breathe the woodsy, moist scent and are equally as eager to set up camp as we are to explore and hang hammocks to dangle in the trees. After a couple of visits, we knew this place needed a name, and a family brainstorming session eventually led us to the perfect one: Camp Cozy.

The name has stuck and become almost a brand in my mind's eye: a plaid thermos filled with wildflowers sits atop our checkered vinyl tablecloth, a pie waits in the car to be pulled out after dinner and sliced around the fire and shared with friends. We will watch sparks fly from the wood, and stars will captivate us with their wonder as the darkness out here is blacker than anything we see at home. Crochet projects, art supplies, and handmade blankets will create the feeling of home away from home.

Time seems to stretch as I move from watching the creek to reading a book, preparing a meal at the picnic table with our trusty Coleman stove, or exploring on a hike. I try to find the same tiny pinecones I gathered one fall but have never seen again. I see the sliding rock that our children have enjoyed, and I take pictures that captivate me with the beauty of the leaves changing. I sit on a picnic bench with my back to the table, an afghan stretched around my shoulders, and a cup of cocoa nestled in my hands. A stump-turned-table serves me as it holds a little pumpkin I brought from home, a candle, and a leaf I collected on a walk.

In the summer, Queen Anne's lace has been snipped from the side of the road somewhere along the way, and a little felt pennant bearing the title "Camp Cozy" is glued to a dowel and slid in with the bouquet. This place seems to get me – it explodes with things that inspire, and it invites a slowness that is restful and welcoming. I pull out my beauty box packed with supplies that I can enjoy when feeling creative or inspired: vintage Jell-O molds for holding nature goodies or candles, twine and scissors for stringing up leaves as a garland, or paper for creating a bunting to tie on sticks and decorate our pie!

Giving places a name gives their memories a place to dwell. It brings validity to the meaning of the place and creates a common entity we can all refer to. We no longer have to explain where we are going camping; we simply state the obvious – Camp Cozy. It has no electricity, no running water, and nothing in the way of modern convenience or comfort. Yet we have found ways to make it feel homey, warm, cozy, and inviting. Each year I look forward to going back to this special place and resting, feasting my eyes, and filling up my heart for the days ahead.

CAMP COZY

Blueberries

At least a decade ago, a dear friend gave us six blueberry bushes. They were starting a farm and offered a gift of the few extra bushes they had. Knowing nothing, we planted them in excitement and gratefulness. As the years have gone by, we really haven't taken very good care of them. We don't know when to prune them, and the weeds have wrapped their arms over, around, and through all the branches, and yet the bushes continue to be a place of haven and nourishment.

Watching the little white blooms pop out in the spring is always a surprise and delight that feels like an unexpected grace – we know we haven't worked for the gift of those blooms and the promise of the fruit to come. Birds must think these branches are a grace, too, for we have two nests snuggled in the inner places. What a delightful place to have a nest! Shielded with small leaves, decorated with flowers, and eventually providing a sweet treat to little beaks – that is a wise mama bird!

Late June arrives, and the little green berries have grown larger and begun to turn pinkish, then purplish, and then the deep blue and purple we have come to recognize as a blueberry. Despite the oppressive heat, and in an effort to cover as much skin as possible so as to avoid becoming a meal for the mosquitoes, I pull on long pants, long sleeves, and my thrifted black rubber boots with gold stars on them. Almost as soon as it is light, I grab a green enamel pan and traipse through the weeds to seek the little treasures hanging in bunches, weighing down the branches.

The purplish berries piled in the green pan are so beautiful and inspiring. The birds chatter and swoop overhead, no doubt displeased at my harvesting their breakfast. Eager to get back into the cool of the air conditioning, I move through the task quickly. Upon completion, I pour the berries into a turquoise colander under cold running water to rinse. My daughter awakens and is eager to pop a handful of fresh berries in her mouth. The sun rises on another day, and we find that to be an undeserved grace as well.

Nature Goodies

Pinecones.

Moss.

Acorns.

Leaves.

A butterfly wing.

Smooth rock.

Prickly gumball.

Dried flowers.

Leaf skeletons.

Evergreen clippings.

Wildflowers.

Twigs.

Mushrooms.

An abandoned nest.

Egg shell from a hatched bird.

Feathers.

Seeds and pods.

Shells.

Berries.

Nuts.

Buds.

Fungus.

Fern fronds.

Tendrils.

Petals.

A woven basket dangling from my arm houses a lovely collection of God's delights that are sprinkled generously through His creation. As a young child, I remember my mom handing me a paper bag at the park on a Sunday afternoon and encouraging me to collect nature goodies. A little friend with us wore a fuzzy blue Cookie Monster coat, and together we frolicked through the park and found treasures.

I've never stopped collecting wonders. Like leaves or flowers pressed in the pages of a book, so are little memories pressed on the pages of my mind. They may be one-dimensional now and a little faded and fragile, but they still retain the essence of beauty that inspired me in the first place.

Things like my children on a walk, picking up prickly gumballs and calling them croutons for their nature salads made just for play. Mud castle creations and hobbit homes adorned with every bloom, berry, and branch found in the yard. Or the time we swapped nature goodies in egg cartons with friends and then admired, observed, and painted these little wonders of creation.

There was the Christmas I was sad not to be traveling to be with family, and a Christmas Eve treasure hunt procured moss, leaves, and pinecones that adorned our dinner table. There have been buckets of shells and armfuls of pinecones collected, and we have examined each one to marvel at the detail and variety of God's handiwork.

Rare treasures are piled into a small chipboard box in our girls' room to be pulled out when special friends come over. Leaves dipped in wax to preserve their color. Evergreen clippings woven into garlands to adorn and make our home festive for Christmas.

These free little treasures are beyond simple and usually ever so small. But they speak of a Creator so attentive to detail, so creative, and so set on delighting us with His artistry. Whether in paper bags or woven baskets, nature salads or chipboard boxes, may I never grow out of collecting nature goodies!

Queen Anne's Lace

My daughter, Rachel, and I volunteer at a local thrift shop about once a week. The dark brick building is on a busy corner, and the sandy parking lot always boasts a bumpy entry. One spring morning, we peeked out the back door to collect some new donations and begin the work of sorting, pricing, and placing items out for sale.

There to my left was a weathered dark green coil of hose, and as the sunlight filtered through the trees, it was a marvelous beauty to see small wild daisies popping up amongst the webbing. In an unlikely back alley, but near the hope of water, these flowers put on a glorious display. They expected no applause and they had no tending. They were just there to be appreciated by anyone willing to notice.

I like to call this side-of-the-road beauty. The kind that is unplanned, haphazard, and not born in ideal conditions. Whizzing down the interstate, a blur of purple begins to form in the median, and pretty soon a swath of yellow catches my eye on the side. A pair of scissors dwells in our glove box for just such occasions, and I've stopped too many times to count to cut weeds from the side of the road. Yes, weeds. That is how many see them: allergy-inducing weeds.

To me, though, they are pure beauty. I imagine the courage it takes to grow near hot, smelly asphalt and noisy hurrying cars. Picture the lack of comfort – and dare I say joy – at being planted near a metal cattle guard rather than in a lush cottage garden. Wildflowers are pure gift. They pop up in the most unlikely places, and they don't care. They are no respecter of where to grow for the most visual enjoyment of their blooms or the most dashing display of delightful color.

One of my favorites to watch for is Queen Anne's lace. The appropriately named lacy blooms on tall, wispy stems grace the sides of interstates from the South all the way into the Midwest. Each summer, I hope to cut a bouquet of these beauties from the side of the road. My great-grandma, affectionately named Memee, had Queen Anne's lace in her wedding bouquet. Whenever I slide the delicate stems into a vintage thermos or canning jar, I savor kinship with family as I celebrate the joy of beauty in unexpected places.

Boat Landing

Less than a mile from our house is an old bridge-turned-boat landing, sprawling alongside a mile-wide river combining fresh and salt water. Birds skitter about and skim the water looking for dinner. Tiny little crabs play hide-and-seek amongst the rocks. The waves *lap, lap, lap* where they meet sand and shells inviting children to explore, collect goodies, and press their toes into the grains. Breeze rustles my hair and keeps the bugs mercifully away from me as I sit and take it all in.

The sun moves through the sky – a golden orb that frames our hours, days, and seasons. The sky looks like a watercolor painting where God's invisible brush paints in cotton-candy hues of pink, purple, blue, and orange. It is living artwork that changes moment by moment as the sun makes its descent toward the horizon, where our view of it will be at rest until the next morning. Each moment seems more beauty-filled than the one before.

The floating dock rises and falls with the tide, the salt smell of the water greets me, the gulls chatter and squawk, and a few weeds grow nearby that I have been known to cut and bring home for a bouquet. Once in a while we may see a dolphin or a boat coming in for the night. It is a heavenly art show every morning and evening, just waiting for me to come and participate in the raising of glory and worship to God.

The light and warmth on my face as it turns toward the sun, the sparkling pathway of light across the water, and the swish and bubble of the waves mesmerize me. I clasp my hands around my knees, and my eyes are squinty from the brightness of the sky. Cars whiz by on the bridge, but for me time stands still, marked only by the lowering of the sun.

Invitations to Imagine

Story and Sip

Heavy wooden doors open as I step into a lovely coffee shop and bookstore. The gray skies outside only enhance the glow from within; lamps are scattered in every nook and cranny. Tapestry armchairs sagging from use offer an invitation as music wafts gently through the background and the aroma of treats dances on the air.

The walls are lined with the most amazing shelves, filled to overflowing with all sorts of enticing reads. I step up to the counter and order my daughter's favorite – a London Fog latte – which perfectly fits the aesthetic of the day and is a delight to order because of its charming name. A mix of tea and frothed milk is placed on the counter, and I am drawn to a corner chair near a tall antique window.

The windows look out over the street, where passersby hurry to get out of the rain. Window boxes spilling over with red geraniums and ivy trailing over the sides create a border of beauty. I slip off one shoe and tuck my foot up under my legs, take a sip of the brew, and let warmth and comfort settle over me. My breathing starts to slow down, and I am curious to watch others gathered here.

The scent of old books is compelling, and the hardcovers speaking of days gone by invite me to turn in my chair and gaze over the titles, looking for a cover to crack open. With my tweed skirt, thick cable-knit tights, corduroy blazer, and my hair pulled back into a wispy knot, I stand and journey over to the shelves for a closer look.

Old friends stand next to each other: Elizabeth Bennett, Jo March, and Anne Shirley. I might even take a look at the children's books, which reminds me of checking books out of the school library at Roosevelt Elementary and falling in love with *Caddie Woodlawn*, *Strawberry Girl*, and *Ramshackle Roost*.

Stories hold memories – it might bring back where we were when we first read the book, or bring to mind certain images through the corridors of time. I might think of evenings perched on our living room couch as a little girl with my mom reading *Little House on the Prairie* and Janette Oke's series to us before bed. Or it may remind me of reading aloud to my own children and making all the different accents and voices in the beloved *The Amazing Tales of Max & Liz* series, reading outside on a summer's night in Colorado with the stars twinkling overhead, or even in a tent on a camping trip.

Running my hand along the shelf and over the spines, I realize that even without opening a book today, I have still walked into the pages of a story – it just so happens that the story is mine, and the corridors of time are the portals to another place that I once knew. A deep and contented sigh escapes my throat and relaxes my shoulders as I make my way across the aged rugs back to my corner seat.

The day is growing later as I slip on my shoe, slide my arms into coat sleeves, and get ready to unfold my umbrella. The atmosphere has wrapped me in a warm glow that will follow me out the door as I re-enter real life.

Kingdom Outpost

This pair of words has emerged in numerous ways for me lately. I can't take credit for the phrase, yet I acknowledge how it has captivated my imagination. It has popped up on Instagram, been mentioned in a sermon, come up in a conversation with a friend in another state, and been spotted in an article. Suddenly, I'm aware of it everywhere, and I love thinking about it!

When I picture an outpost, my mind goes to a thickly wooded, remote area with a little cabin in it. The cabin is rustic but snug, and light glows from the windows as smoke wisps up from the chimney. There is life inside and it is inviting, warm, and safe. Words like *haven*, *refuge*, and *shelter* come to mind.

To a weary traveler trudging along, that first speck of light spotted through the trees must ignite a bloom of hope in the heart. It is the first flicker and spark of possibility where things may have seemed hopeless. The longing for food, shelter, companionship, and peace compels the traveler to take a risk. As she fumbles to the door, she wonders what she will find inside, but the light is too compelling to pass up.

Those who live inside would happily open the door to a stranger, pour a bowl of soup, wrap a blanket around the shivering shoulders of their guest, and wrap hands around a steaming mug of something tasty and warming. They would pull up an extra chair and lean forward in eagerness to find out more about who has come to their door and how they can help.

Most likely, very few of us live in a rustic cabin, yet our homes and lives can be just such an outpost for the kingdom of heaven! When the light of Christ fills our hearts, there is a glow that pours forth from us like that first speck of light to a weary traveler in search of help. We have the Gospel available to hold out the light of hope to anyone willing to listen and receive. Yes, we are sometimes able to offer a hot meal or a cup of cold water as well, but nothing could be sweeter than the meeting of physical needs leading to an opportunity to feed the soul as well. May our lives become Kingdom outposts, O Lord, extending Your hope, home, and healing to a weary world!

Monica Wilkinson

Weathered Barns

From the dark pavement of the interstate, weathered barns catch my eye as we pass farms and fields. The stories they could tell captivate my imagination, and I wonder so many things about them. Who thought to build a barn in that exact spot years ago? What animals were cared for inside? When was the last time someone went inside?

Red, white, brown – abandoned barns seem a dime a dozen, yet they call to me in their silent charm. The older and more weathered, the more compelling the barn seems. There's the rustic scent of earth and time, the way the light pours in through the windows and illuminates dust particles dancing in the shadowy corners. Barns are often in open spaces, down cute roads, and in picturesque fields.

My imagination is alive as I picture a summer picnic on a farm-y table with a textured backdrop of chippy paint and worn wood. A soft, aged quilt would cover the table, and it would be set with enamel dishes and pottery bowls that have stories of their own. Perhaps the menu would include chicken salad, homemade bread, chilled slices of watermelon, a layer cake, and lemonade. A bouquet of wildflowers would adorn the center, gathered in the warmth of waving grass as the breeze teases my hair. A canning jar would fit right in as their vase.

Or maybe it would be a fall gathering to celebrate and give thanks for the harvest. An evening that gets dark earlier with a hint of chill in the air and the scent of campfire and decaying leaves. Pumpkins, mums, a warm pot of soup, and some hot cider would be perfect. Family and friends may gather around on hay bales to laugh, talk, and exclaim over the stars. Plaid blankets piled in a basket would be ready to pull over cold legs or wrap around shivering shoulders.

During winter, the gathering might be inside the barn, offering a shelter from wind and cold. White twinkle lights would dangle overhead as they add magic and delight. Plaid thermoses on a side table might hold hot chocolate and a vintage muffin tin would hold peppermint sticks, marshmallows, and whipped cream. A faint hint of hay would lace the air stirring my heart to remember the stable that housed our dear Jesus's birth. Tables would make a center line through the barn, layered with plaids, evergreen, cranberries, and candles – the whole atmosphere dancing with sparkling anticipation of the Christmas season.

As spring begins to emerge, maybe a breakfast picnic takes place on a quilt outside the barn. The first blooms snipped would provide a graceful beauty to the gathering. A feeling of hope would arise as nature awakens from a time of rest and sleep. New life would emerge to remind us that seasons are a gift. God is so wise and so good – look! A bird is hunting for worms to share with her babies, the first butterfly of the year dances by, and there is a slight warmth beginning in the air.

My imagination has run away with me, thinking of all the fun ideas – a beckoning to slow down and savor. To receive the gift of time and well-worn grace that has weathered many storms and still stands as a place of welcome and gathering.

Glow from the Windows

Dusk begins to fall
Family returns
From busy work of day
To the quiet peace of home

Evening settles in
Lights begin to glow
Hearts are calmed and stilled
What a joy to be at home

Gather for a meal
Share about our day
Tend to daily tasks
Let nighttime have her way

Warmth begins within
As we welcome loved ones home
Giving thanks and cozy hugs
And putting slippers on

Hanging up the keys
Putting things away
It's time to settle in
And begin to close the day

From outside these walls
People passing by
An inviting glow
Beckons nosy eyes

Driving down the street
Wondering what's inside
Catching just a glimpse
Of beauty and of life

Glow from the windows
Tells us someone's home
Makes us wonder and
Imagine what lives behind that glow

Are others warmly welcomed there
As the light bids us come close
Is there joy and laughter
Or rather sorrow and no hope

Let our homes be a beacon
A lighthouse to the world
Inviting others to the warmth
That all God's children know

Let this light shine bright
For everyone to see
To come and know the gentle glow
Of God's great family

He's knocking at the door
Won't you invite Him in
He's more than just a one-time guest
He's a forever friend

Let the windows of my heart
Also cast a glow
Inviting those around me
To the Father that I know

Monica Wilkinson

Refuge on Wheels

It's Wednesday evening, and I'm sitting in the car during youth group. Rain is gently pattering against the roof of the car and tap dancing on the windshield. The gray sky and arrival of night create a cozy cocoon inside, and I feel enveloped in a peaceful place. Who knew a Honda Pilot could be a sanctuary from the crazy of the world – but it can and it has many times.

Perhaps my car has become more of a haven since the quarantine because we've had picnics in the car and taken drives just because. It has become a way of seeing things and expanding horizons even when we have limitations from a pandemic. It is what I've been known to call a "sanctuary on wheels" as it becomes a place of worship, prayer, and catching up with loved ones, or a place to practice a verse I'm trying to memorize, process thoughts, and let my heart rest.

As the sky darkens, the light from downtown windows becomes brighter. The street lights' glow intensifies, and the watery reflections on the pavement take on sparkles of light. The party lights strung over a brick patio in our quaint downtown area look whimsical through the old oak trees and draping Spanish moss.

As light fades, the feeling of safety in my little nest on wheels becomes more pronounced. I am grateful to be in out of the rain, with feet tucked underneath me and my rain jacket providing an extra layer of warmth. The rain drops on the windshield sparkle as they trickle down the slope, and the shapes they create change every moment as a new drop of water falls and joins them.

It's actually rather magical. I had considered driving home and back instead of sitting here and waiting, but I'm so glad I brought things to do and carved out space to just be tonight. To reflect and enjoy the simple gift of today. The gift of the rain. The gift of the lights glowing. The gift of feeling cozy and comfortable in this serene and almost reverent moment in time.

OBJECTS IN MIRROR ARE
CLOSER THAN THEY APPEAR

Cute Roads

It has become a family thing to call out "cute road" while on a road trip, or even when we're just out for the day. I often exclaim over this or that being qualified for the title—like a driveway tucked in the woods with a rustic wooden gate, or a little tree-lined lane whose entrance is barely visible from the main road.

To be honest, I'm not entirely sure what qualifies as a cute road unless I see it and it just speaks to me. But I can say this – cute roads are usually gravel, they are hidden, and they offer mystery and an invitation to imagine what is down the lane. Cute roads are tucked away; they curve out of view and spark the desire to wonder what is hidden around the corner or behind the crumbling stone wall.

Sun streams through the trees, and it is easy to wander through the visions in my mind to a cute cottage with smoke coming out of the chimney, or perhaps an open field of wildflowers with a fallen log where I can sit and enjoy the quiet beauty of the afternoon. Maybe the road leads to a wooded path where a slow walk would provide the spicy scent of evergreen, the crunch of leaves underfoot, the moist smell of earth and moss, and the occasional flutter of a bird overhead.

Of course, it is possible that the appearance of these roads gives is completely misleading, but since I don't actually know what lies on the other side the ending is up to my creative inspiration. Frequently, cute roads are not actually accessible – they are visible from the interstate but have a private drive sign. But it doesn't really seem to matter that I can't experience the cute road for myself when the invitation of seeing it is enough to delight my senses and spark my imagination.

Heavenly Homeland

Home should be the coziest place there is. It is the place we can be our true selves – the place where we put on our stretchy pants and don't worry about who sees us, where we can have bed-head and know that those who share the space with us still love us anyway (thankfully)!

Home is the place where we make memories, serve warm meals on cold nights, have picnics in the backyard, and gather around the Christmas tree. Home is a place of comfort and a delight to our senses. It is the place we cultivate growth and change, and the place where we sit quietly in prayer. But we all know and have experienced that our earthly homes will disappoint us – wood rots and needs to be replaced, unkind words are spoken and need to be forgiven, pipes get old and brittle and weeding is a never-ending task.

None of these wearying things are waiting for us in our heavenly homeland. Quite the opposite, in fact! God tells us many things about the home He is preparing for us there, but the main thing is we will be with Him. What could be better?

The truest part of ourselves – our souls – will finally be free to experience life in all its fullness for His glory and praise. There will be feasting and fellowship, singing and worship. There will be light and color, and the very obvious absence of sin, death, and disease. What kind of longing does this cultivate in your heart?

I love God's use of home in His Word to both call us now and prepare us for the future.

In Revelation, He talks of standing at the door of our hearts and knocking. He wants to come in, but He will not push His way in. He is waiting for an invitation, an opening of the door, a welcome – He longs to take a seat at the table, enjoy a bowl of something warm, look deeply into our eyes and hearts, and listen to anything and everything we want to tell Him.

He tells us that we are in a foreign land right now, and that our true citizenship is not in this home, but in a home to come. He is waiting to welcome us to this heavenly homeland, where we will finally experience true rest. We will worship like never before, and we will never stop. The way God has wired us will be evident, and we will feel more alive than we have ever experienced, all in the presence of our dear Savior.

I cannot even imagine or put into words the longing, hope, and joy that will be fulfilled in that warmest welcome Home ever. The earthly joy we feel in being welcomed home by warmth, preparation, and little touches of care will be blown out of the water in our true Home. If coziness is defined as "giving a feeling of comfort, warmth, and relaxation," – then our eternal address will be cozier than we can even dream up right now with our limited experience and understanding. But God – He is capable of so much more than we can imagine, and just like a loving father, He delights in bringing a smile to our face and wrapping us in His love!

Farmhouse

Down a curvy, tree-lined dirt lane, the porch stretches wide and welcoming. A pasture and cottage garden create a magazine-worthy view off to the side as I pull up the drive. Wooden rockers with pillows in them beckon a pause, a glass of lemonade, and a catch-up chat. Planters overflowing with red geraniums create a cheery contrast to the white wood planks that make up the siding. A dog sleeps lazily on one end of the porch, and his tail wags in greeting while the rest of him stays put – very content in his napping position.

The heavy wooden door cracks open, and the aroma of freshly baked bread and something with cinnamon waft out to add their welcome to the symphony of invitations bombarding my senses. A comfy rug awaits just inside to cushion bare and sock feet, layering another greeting to the open door's invitation to come in, rest awhile, relax, and be at home.

Worn hardback books fill the shelves, and cozy corners beckon me to sit and put my feet up to read. Chippy shiplap and old-house woodwork are the perfect canvas of patina and charm. Lamps and fading sunlight fill the rooms with a glow that speaks to what is blooming in my heart as I slip off my shoes and step into this dream world.

The kitchen boasts schoolhouse light fixtures, handcrafted rolling pins, crockery, and a calico apron. There is the source of the hints of cinnamon I've been smelling – an apple pie quietly rests on a sideboard, and my mouth can hardly wait to taste it. A pot of soup simmers on the stovetop and candlelight dances on the table already set for dinner. Hands are washed, prayers of thanks lifted up, and smiles shared as chairs glide across the timeworn floors. Soup is ladled into bowls, thick slices of bread are slathered with butter, and flowers in canning jars enchant me with their beauty as I soak in every detail and how it delights my senses.

This is a world where patchwork quilts grace each of the beds, and stairs that creak and moan only add to the charm and character of the house. I head to bed early, laying my head on feather pillows and tucking feet into crisp sheets underneath the softness of a well-worn quilt. Morning will come soon enough, and there will be eggs to gather, flowers to cut, and clothes to hang on the line.

The farmhouse has that feeling of a visit with a friend. It has known hardship, struggle, joy, and laughter, and still offers love and acceptance. It offers cozy comfort, a shelter from stormy days, and a haven for the homesick. The patina that comes with age only adds to its character and beauty.

As the sun slips out of sight and the comfort and loveliness of home sink deep into my bones, I know the feeling of being known, wanted, and safe. The farmhouse opens her arms wide and exposes her flaws and heart while offering a warm, inviting welcome to just come and be yourself, and I fall asleep feeling right at home.

Sparkles of Lights

This past year, I read a book entitled *Adorning the Dark* by Andrew Peterson. This simple trio of words has captivated me: Adorn the Dark – let them roll around in your heart and mind and ask yourself where do they resonate with you? Where do they land? How do they beckon a response?

To adorn is to make more beautiful or attractive, and we all know the darkness we are faced with in our world each day. Think of all the adorning we do at the darkest time of year – winter. Think especially of the lights – lights on trees and homes, candles bringing a glow to tables, young and old gathering around a warm and cheering fire, watching the reflections of light across the snow and ice.

Adorning the dark is not giving victory to the darkness. It is giving whispers of beauty to a world that desperately needs to see the Light of the World.

Winter is known as a season of darkness and can feel empty and long at times. Sunset arrives earlier and the evening and night stretch long before the sun peeks up over the surface of the horizon again. It is a season of cocooning and staying in, a time where the earth seems barren. It is during this season that we can be beauty hunters looking for ¬– and creating – places of light.

We find and share light in the simple act of lighting of a candle or the ordinary sharing of a meal, looking to our faith and extending grace and kindness in thousands of big and small ways. In each of these ways and more, we put out little sparkles of light that dance in the darkness around us.

Why is light so compelling? Light is warm and inviting; it speaks of life and says that someone is home and waiting for you. As you are driving home, light shines from windows, and you can see the sweet simplicity of belonging and warmth spilling out of the windows.

A warm fire is not only comforting to your chilled body, but delights with its ever-changing light. Watching the sparks dance and fly, watching the embers smoldering as air hits them, and seeing the smiles on those gathered around the fire brings light to your eyes as well.

Have you ever been out in a very dark place at night and seen how amazing the stars are? The darker our surroundings, the more powerful one little speck of light can be.

Light is easily multiplied – when one spark of light is present, others are inspired to reach out and start their own spark of light. Lighting one candle from another is like receiving a kindness and then desiring to pass that to someone else. Light spreads, and when it does, its beauty and impact become greater and more visible. This is the cumulative impact of what it would visually look like if each of us offered a single spark of light even once. As it rapidly multiplies, we see that the darkness is fading and light is delighting our senses and decorating the lives of those we hold near.

With Advent upon us, we think of light maybe more this time of year than any other, and maybe those who don't yet know this light will be more receptive because it is the season of light.

We watch the lights of the Advent candles get brighter each week as we approach the celebration of the ultimate adorning of the dark that happened over two thousand years ago when the Light of the World stepped away from the place where pure, holy light radiates from every crevice of heaven and came to this earth, where the throne of darkness seems to get darker and darker each day. The events of that adorning have rolled and surged through history, and yes, even through us as our display of light connects us like millions of branches on the eternal family tree, tracing its roots all the way to the source of True Light and compelling us to follow His beautiful example.

Matthew 5:14-16 reminds us that we are, "the light of the world. A city set on a hill cannot be hidden. Nor do people light a lamp and put it under a basket, but on a stand, and it gives light to all in the house. In the same way, let your light shine before others, so that they may see your good works and give glory to your Father who is in heaven."

This is the cumulative impact of what it would visually look like if each of you offered a single spark of light even once. You can see how this multiplies rapidly as we repeat this offering again and again and again throughout our lifetimes.

How will you give yourself to the adorner of the dark this Advent as we anticipate and celebrate with joy His coming and arrival to adorn our lives with light in every season?

The Refuge and Realness of Home

Fading Light

One of my favorite endings to a slow afternoon is to watch the light fade and grow dim while we keep the lights low in our home. This is hard to do when others are around, because they frequently want to turn lights on and not fumble around in the dark! But once in a while, it happens where everyone is occupied or I'm home alone, and I can enjoy the welcome to evening in a gentle and peaceful way.

It has kind of become a joke that I am always turning lights down and off. I don't really know how to explain it, but it feels very calm and peaceful to me for the lights to be low and not harsh. Even so, what I'm describing in fading light is even more than just turning down the lights.

Afternoon sun streams through the French doors that lead to our screened-in porch. I'm sitting at one end of the dining room table, working on a little of this and a little of that or reading a magazine. Pretty soon, the golden hour starts to change the light as it is honeyed and pinkish in the sky, therefore reflecting such colors into our kitchen and dining room. The sky looks like watercolors through the trees.

This is a great time to light a candle, because soon, the sun will dip below the horizon, and that soft dusk will permeate our home. I don't mind just sitting still and enjoying how every moment, the light changes and darkens as night descends on our side of the earth.

A small lamp perched on the kitchen windowsill provides just enough light to navigate fixing a cup of tea, but then I'm happy to sit in the semi-darkness some more. What is it that is so enjoyable about the fading of the light into night?

It feels soft, there is no fanfare and no noise – just the consistent rhythm and predictability of the day turning to evening turning to night. It is an opportunity to choose quiet, calm, and peace. To keep the outside world outside and just enjoy the simplicity and solitude of watching the light and feeling the evening envelop our home in quiet, stillness, and rest. It is the pause and deep breath that lasts more than two seconds that our souls need.

Pretty soon, I may wander into the bedroom and turn on a lamp, but I will carry with me the gift of slowing down to enjoy the fading light.

The Yellow Apartment

Nestled in a neighborhood of vintage bungalows, there is a collection of buildings painted yellow. I had always thought they were cute, but in my single days, I imagined that the rent would be higher than I could pay, even with a roommate.

Upon finding out that the house we'd been renting for a couple of years was going up for sale, a fellow roomie and I decided to check out the yellow apartments, and in the loveliest turn of events, they were a great deal.

We moved into an upstairs unit, and that place became my first real experience at creating a cozy home of my own. It was not the first place I lived on my own, but the first place where I began to truly embrace who I was and develop my style while curating a home that was both lovely and inviting. Most elements were thrifted, free or handmade, and it was a haven of peace to me for a few years.

The wide tile windowsills held candles in the winter that created magic on Christmas Eve. Retro black and yellow tiles in the bathroom seemed tricky at first, yet I grew to love the look with black and white photos and a fabric skirt hot glued to the porcelain sink. One Christmas Eve, I even floated candles in the bathtub to add charm and a warm glow.

The windows cranked open with old handles, and aside from the fact that my curtains fluttered with a draft even when the windows were closed, I loved their charm. It was in the yellow apartment that I hosted a waffle picnic on the green picnic table in the open space next to my building. I left tin cans with flowers in them by the mailboxes for my neighbors on May Day. I hosted a tea party for my mom's birthday one year and made notecards that expressed delightful characteristics of each guest to give as gifts.

The galley kitchen was tiny, but it was also where I got my taste of canning, windows propped open a bit for some cool fresh air while the aroma of apples processing filled my heart and home to the full. My creativity expanded greatly in this little space – making quilts out of old pairs of jeans and gifting them to friends getting married or having babies, giving dessert of the month to a couple of special people, beginning to collect vintage and thrifted finds and enjoying this little nest to the fullest.

This has lingered as a special place in my memory. This was the place where I think I realized who I was. Just after moving in, I started a new job at a place that remains very dear to me – it was influential in my spiritual growth but also fed my love and appreciation of beauty and slowing down before I even realized these things about myself.

Thank you, little yellow apartment, for being a haven, a training ground, and a place to discover myself and embrace the gifting God has placed in my heart.

happy
May
day!
d.

Jammies

Comfy and cozy
Relaxing and soft
Shedding the daytime
I turn my brain off

Slow down my body
And quiet my heart
Finding rest at home
A lost, dying art

Jammies invite me
To set cares aside
To welcome the joy
And quiet of night

Be kind to yourself
There's only one you
Put on your jammies
Your spirit renewed

Turn down the lights
And tuck under a quilt
Refresh and restore
Instead of just wilt

Sip some warm tea or
Pull out a good book
Enjoy company
In a cozy nook

Invite yourself home
Be truly yourself
And don't worry for
The clock on the shelf

Be kind to yourself
There's only one you
Put on your jammies
Your spirit renewed

Light from a candle
And warmth from the glow
Whispering music
To your ears will flow

Walk in the door
Go straight to your room
Put on your jammies
Let slow and rest bloom

Jammies feel like a
Warm comforting hug
Sock feet resting on
A soft fluffy rug

Be kind to yourself
There's only one you
Put on your jammies
Your spirit renewed

Now is the time to
Crawl into your bed
To pull up the sheets
And lay down your head

Tomorrow will come
A day fresh and new
But your need for rest
Is both tried and true

Quiet your heart and
Softly whisper prayer
Let Him bring you peace
In His gentle care

Be kind to yourself
There's only one you
Put on your jammies
Your spirit renewed

A Candle on the Porch

Years ago, I was invited to stay in the home of a friend of my sister. One of the things I noticed about being in her home was how warm and cozy the lighting was. In the evenings, she had little electric candle lights, lamps, and even a candle in a mason jar on the porch, where a worn and comfy quilt waited patiently on the bench.

Sitting on the porch that night in the crisp air and covered up with the quilt, I thought this was the most magical evening I could remember in a long time. It was well into spring, but still a time where a quilt was needed, and the candle provided warmth to my eyes and heart. That was an evening that I didn't want to end, for I knew when I got up it would break the spell of inspiration and joy that had delighted my spirit.

Through the years, I've thought of this atmosphere with fondness and a desire to replicate it. When my children were young, I noticed that large overhead lights were not only harsh but invited a more energetic mood, whereas smaller, warmer lights created a mood of quieting, of peace, of lowering our voices and calming our hearts.

Perhaps this is one reason I love gray days so much – it makes the light so warm and inviting, so soft and calming inside. The gray outside beckons me to bake, pull out a favorite book or magazine, slowly sip a cup of tea, and enjoy a variety of other beauty-cultivating and cozy activities.

I've been known to sit in a dark room with only a candle for light, make breakfast by candlelight, walk through rooms and turn lights off, add twinkly lights to our table, and yes, even light a candle and set it out on my porch.

Just as a candle on the porch is extravagant and superfluous, it is also a generous greeting and welcome. I want this feeling and emotion to grace my home and life – when others enter my presence or are greeted at my door, may it be with just such a generous and warm welcome where they feel they can put their feet on the coffee table and press one of the slouchy pillows into just the right position to relax and be comfy.

Imagine walking or driving by windows at night. We hope to catch a peek at the warmth and comfort of a family inside, just doing ordinary things like cleaning up the dinner table or folding the laundry or straightening the couch cushions. The warmth of the light is inviting and the life inside connects us to one another.

A candle on the porch is the same thing – it is so cozy, and it speaks of life and invitation, warmth and hospitality. Somehow if we were to see a candle on the porch, we would just know in our souls that a kindred spirit lives within who would welcome us with a smile, an invitation to sit, and probably even something to drink.

A candle on the porch is a reason to slow down and just be, for no reason at all and with no agenda. May we invite not only guests, but ourselves as well, with such tender gracefulness and joy.

The
Haunted
Theatre

Gray Days

It is no secret in my house that gray is one of my favorite colors. This love of gray started with a delight over gray days. I love it when the sky is overcast and everything inside feels cozy. Lights glow warmer, candlelight is more delightful, and I want to read a book, bake, and enjoy all the homey things.

On a trip to France years ago, I noticed how everything was gray. The sky, water, and coastline were gray, and the houses were varying shades of neutrals and beige. What stood out to me even more was the fact that the gardens shone all the brighter because of the gray backdrop. A bloom of pink was glorious against the quietness of all the neutral tones.

Just as the simple blooms and greens of growing things seemed brilliant on those gray days, so the ordinary little things of our lives can be magnified in beauty against the backdrop of a gray, cozy day.

Cloudy days invoke a feeling of peace, a glow from the windows of our homes, a desire to pull in and be comfy. To ladle out a bowl of soup or a toasty grilled cheese sandwich, to brew a cup of hot tea or turn on the twinkle lights. To curl up with a movie or great book or linger slowly over a puzzle.

The softer light is calming and puts my heart in a place of graceful quiet. My slippers are tucked up under me on the couch as I get cozy and enjoy the gift of the day. I want to take photos of the moody light and capture the feeling so I can remember it on other days. The backdrop of a gray, cozy day can be a beautiful canvas for savoring simple pleasures that can both warm and spark delight in our hearts.

Patchwork Quilt

My girls' favorite quilt in our home is a handmade patchwork creation that my mom made for me years ago with four inch squares of dresses and clothes from my childhood. Those memories became neighbors with one another when stitched side by side and held together with thread and love.

The fabrics are worn and some are faded. In fact, I almost got rid of this quilt one year – there were so many holes I wondered if it was worth keeping anymore. But the begging and pleading of the girls won out, and my mom volunteered to champion the task of replacing the worn squares.

Perhaps this should be called the memory quilt rather than just patchwork for it is loaded to the brim with not only the fabrics but things I did and experienced while wearing them. I see the purple and white stripes and remember a sun dress, the blue one with tiny rosebuds that was a Christmas dress, and the mint green fabric with peach flowers that my mom made into a blouse I wore on my first airplane flight with my grandma. I see the matching yellow and pink prints made into Easter dresses for my sister and me, and I can picture my hair in tight curls after sleeping on pink foam curlers the night before.

There is the Hollie Hobbie square and the aqua floral print, and the white fabric with strawberries that had been one of my dad's shirts. I remember picking out the peach, yellow, mint, and purple floral print at the fabric store to be made into an Easter dress when I was in junior high.

Some of the prints are faded and holding on by a few threads, quite literally.

Some are more vibrant from recent replacing. The inside batting has seen better days and in some places has disintegrated and washed away over the years. But none of that seems to matter in a treasure like this. Regardless of any of its physical difficulties, my girls still gently fight over whose turn it is to use it. And if they are sick, this is the quilt most requested to provide comfort and peace.

It is possible to look back over my life and see similar things. Some pieces are vibrant and colorful, still holding strong, while others are faded, worn thin, and not of much use anymore. The threads of life are held together and are stronger when pieced next to each other and seen as a work of art and beauty adding up to a treasure.

It reminds of the tapestry poem shared by Corrie ten Boom which begins with the lines, "My life is but a weaving / between my God and me. / I cannot choose the colors / He weaveth steadily." God takes all the bits and pieces of life, the colorful parts and the faded parts, the strong and the worn thin. He makes them all into something beautiful, something that brings comfort, solace, and peace to others when we share of how He has gently stitched together the frayed edges of our stories.

When we can look for His presence in, around and through our lives, it changes our perspective and softens us with age and use. Softens us to be used for His glory and His kingdom. Just as a quilt softened by age provides extra warmth and comfort, so our lives can become sources of comfort and compassion as we are softened by age and shaped by God's love.

My girls don't really verbalize all of these things when they reach down to pull the pastel calico squares over their frames. They just know that there is a feeling of home and comfort wrapped up in those squares. The quilt represents three generations of our family: Grammie assembled it, I lived the memories, and now my children savor the warmth.

Lord, may You stitch together all the scraps of life, into a legacy of Your love that will provide life and comfort to all who seek refuge under its weight.

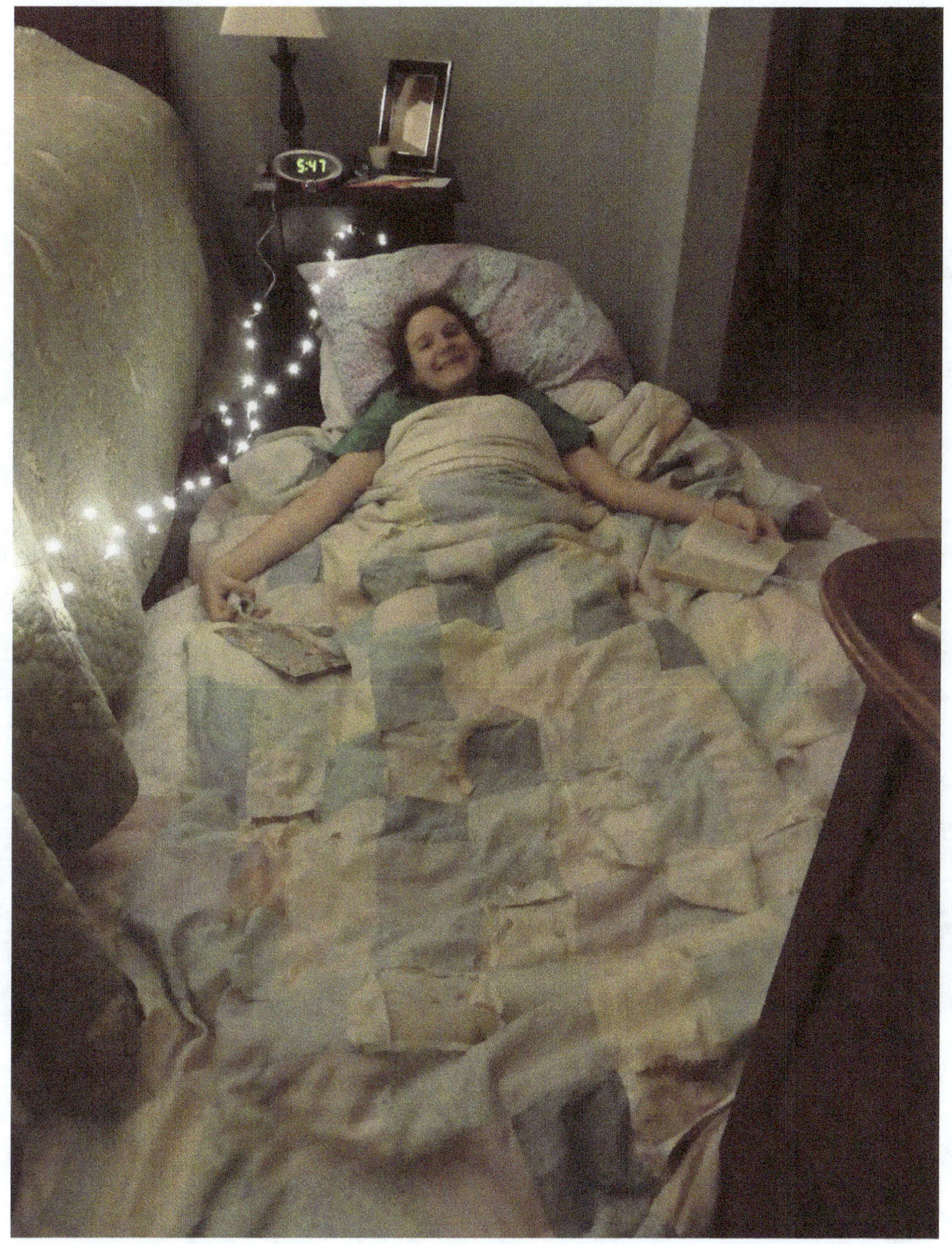

The Attic

Lifting the panel on the opening in our laundry room ceiling leads to the attic that holds things like outgrown baby toys, Christmas decorations, and suitcases for future travel excursions. I try very hard not to ever venture into the attic, always pleading with someone else in my family to do the task instead. But one Thursday morning found me hunting for an outgrown ballet costume to share with my niece, and into the dreaded attic I went.

When I think of attics, I want to picture something out of the *Little Women* movie where charm abounds and inspiration awaits. This is not our attic. To be fair, our attic does what an attic needs to do – it stores things out of the way of everyday life but still within reach for occasional use.

Dragging the ladder in and sliding the ceiling panel aside, I straighten my back and lift my chin. I can do this. Armed with a flashlight and on a mission, I ascend, and the rummaging begins. Because this is not a place I frequent (cough, cough – ever) I'm not familiar with where things are or where to begin looking for the bin holding the outgrown costumes.

Rafters provide some stability as I try not to step in any wrong place, hit my head, or see anything creepy like a dead bug, or worse, a live mouse (shudder). I tentatively peer inside suitcases and boxes, of toys from days gone by – no costume. I look in more boxes but my stamina for staying strong is waning. Not one to easily admit defeat, I come down the ladder, assuming I am just not going to find it or perhaps it isn't there.

I close everything up and put it all away, but my curiosity and desire to delight the birthday girl pushes me to try again. *It has to be up there*, I think to myself.

The entire process repeats: dragging in the ladder, I place one foot in front of the other on the metal rungs with flashlight in hand. It's chilly and dark up there, and my nerves are a bit tight again, hoping I won't see something I don't want to see.

Of course I see all the same boxes that were there ten minutes ago, but I decide to up my investigative game a bit. Boxes marked "china and memorabilia" catch my eye, and before I know it, I've found a plethora of tea-related items all from various family members. Making my way down with my haul, I still have no costume.

Eventually, one of my daughters takes pity on me and agrees to help me look in our second attic over the bedrooms. We figure out that the long-burned-out light merely needs a new bulb, and in our joy over fixing the light, we are invigorated to look with fresh energy. An inspection of this attic turns up empty boxes, sleeping bags, and an animal trap once used to try and catch something scratching around in this very space. Still no costume.

But the fresh energy of youth pursues one last look in the first attic just to see if she can find what my eyes did not. And sure enough, a long flat bin is spotted and filled to the brim with tulle, fluff, sequins, and memories. She exclaims over many costumes, amazed at how tiny she and her sister once were. She calls out which songs went with which costumes, and I marvel at her memory. There in the folds of ribbon and netting is the deep jewel-tone turquoise Arabian-looking outfit we have been searching for. We are elated, and our energy is refreshed at the discovery of our treasure. We can't wait to surprise an Aladdin-loving cousin with this gift!

Shortly after our final venture into the attic, it's time for me, to head to work. I'm somewhat trembly from the whole affair, and not sure how to describe why it is unsettling for me but it is. And though I arrive scattered, I have a powerful visual in my mind of the attic and how it relates to our souls.

It dawns on me that just like it is hard to enter the chaotic, dark, and who-knows-what-we'll-find attic, so it is with being vulnerable with those around me. Maybe I'm afraid that they will see something they wish they hadn't, or that they'll find chaos, dirt, or darkness in me. Yes, rummaging around will likely turn up some things that may be best left hidden away. But there is also the hope of finding treasures and unearthing some great discoveries.

cozy

The Glorious Smallness of Home

Sitting on our screened-in porch one summer evening, it struck me how hidden and small life is inside our home. As with most things, this can have two sides – but I'm thinking about the side full of wonder and joy.

We play a card game and hear the birds sing in the trees. No one else knows what we are doing – it isn't reported on the evening news or disrupting anyone else's home life. The twinkle lights strung overhead glow brighter as the sun sets and the cicadas start their evening symphony.

I imagine how many houses line our street, the neighborhoods, towns, cities, states, and countries – the number is staggering and reminds me of the smallness of home.

This is a blessing somehow, as we just go about ordinary, everyday life without fanfare and without fame. Mundane tasks are made beautiful when done in service to my home and family. Inviting friends and neighbors to share in our home expands our walls for a few hours.

It is like the little bird fluttering about throughout the day to find food and stretch her wings. At night she twirls around and heads back to her little nest. A place of comfort, haven, and rest. A small place, but a place that means the world to her, for it is hers.

Yes, in the grand scheme of things, home is less than a dot in the galaxy. Yet it is such a large part of our lives and our framework for seeing the world. This is where the view of home grows large – in how we welcome, in how we care for and nurture those within our homes (including ourselves!) and in how we use these homes to be a haven from the rest of the world.

We go out into the world to see new things and have grand adventures, but we long to get back to our nest. To fluff our pillows, eat with our own dishes, and sleep in our own beds.

This is why I see glory and delight in the smallness of home – because it is my little speck of the world to come to after a long day or a long trip. It welcomes me in with familiar warmth and comfort. And, while it is humble and far from perfect, it accepts me for just who I am and provides refuge and peace within.

Warm Apple Butter

Hot, sticky days of August come to a close, and it's time to start thinking about the annual trip to the apple orchard several hours away. The day of our trip has arrived, it is afternoon and time to load the car and hit the road with visions of apple cider donuts and a picnic alongside trees laden with orbs of green and red.

Arriving at the rented house, there is always excitement to feel the cooler air of a temperature drop from driving north and to sense the beginning of a seasonal change that has not yet arrived in the coastal town our family calls home. Excitement is high even as bodies slow down and enjoy nature, games, and reading books.

After a night of rest, it is time to wake and pack a picnic. Today's the anticipated day that is looked forward to each year. Familiar exits pass by and the left turn approaches, boasting the sign for the orchard pointing guests to the steep mountain drive. Some years there is a spotting of the first goldenrod for this season on the side of the road and the anticipation of another fall being ushered in, where bouquets will be cut from weedy lots and the stems arranged in a vase for free porch décor. At the top of this small mountain, there are bales of hay, rows of parked cars, school busses of children, and the scent of apples wafting on the breeze.

The large farm stand welcomes with an inviting aroma, mounds of apples, and stacks of baskets lining the wall, waiting for pickers to come and accept the invitation to fill them with sweet treasures. The slushy machine is swirling, and mouths start watering with the anticipation of a cider slushy after warming up in the rows of trees and fruit.

Eagerly, we begin the journey by heading down the hill, though we know that what goes down must come back up later with full baskets and tired legs. After coming for several years, children know just where to go and make a straight line for the rows marked Honeycrisp, Gala, McIntosh, and Pink Lady.

Mounds of soft apples lie underneath each tree, starting to ferment yet still displaying a certain beauty in their heaps. The colors have not yet faded, even if the flesh is less desirable than it was in its crisp state. Piled under trees amidst leaves and tree trunks, the apples are still beautiful even in their dying. Even more inspiring are the rows of trees laden with fruit, beckoning hands to stretch up and pick a few, walk a little, pick a few more, walk a little more. There is always a bit of extra excitement for the apple that detaches with a few leaves still attached, lending the apple extra character and charm! A pocket knife is usually pulled from a teen's pocket, and an apple sliced and shared right there from the tree.

As baskets fill, photos are taken to capture memories of this treasured tradition. Too soon, it seems the load is heavy and no more can be carried. The walk back to the stand always seems longer and steeper than it did earlier in the morning. But there is happiness and stickiness and a readiness for the next part of the adventure, too.

Apples are paid for and loaded into the car, as we quickly unload a picnic lunch and get in line at the donut shack for a dozen wreaths of warm apple cinnamon heavenliness. What could be better than a hot donut whose aroma has been wafting through the air since our arrival this morning? Icy and fresh slushies are carried over in a box, and paper straws from home adorn them with a little love. Oh, that first sip tastes so refreshing! For some, fall is cool and crisp, but in the deep South, the heat of fall is not much less than the full heat of summer, so any little touch of cool is a deep sigh of relief.

In typical beauty-maker fashion, I have packed a table cloth and some pretty things to put on the table, but the one constant is always apples. They are the highlight of the table décor.

Apple trees line one side of the picnic tables, and children happily play on various little houses and climbing things or dig in the sandbox nearby. Lunch is enjoyed, and there is a delight in the joy of being here together again, sometimes with friends along as well.

Next it is time for the hay ride on a tractor that includes no hay, but can't be missed anyway. There is a stop for photos at the *How Tall This Fall* sign – grandparents love seeing the photos of grandkids in front of that sign each year and will be amazed at how much they've grown.

Much too soon, the day is spent, and it won't come back around again until next year. But the enjoyment of apples has only begun. The same dinner is on the menu each year on apple-picking day: applesauce pancakes with bacon or sausage, syrup, and juice or milk. It is the epitome of simple and homey food. Yes, there has been eating of apple things all day, but that never seems to matter. A basket or bowl of apples with little twinkle lights tucked in and around is likely gracing the center of the table.

And the next morning, it is time to go home. This is where the work begins. Apples are diced for the freezer to use in muffins and oatmeal, apple pie filling is bubbling on the stove, and yes, warm apple butter is simmering. A favorite method is to peel and quarter the apples in the evening, then put them in the Crockpot all night. Slumbering bodies awake to the sweet smell of warm apples and the hope that in a few more hours it will be ready to taste!

Soon the lid is removed, spices and sugar are stirred in, and the immersion blender whizzes everything into a smooth cinnamon-colored liquid that smells like fall and Christmas and home all wrapped up in one. I go out to the mailbox just so I can have the excuse to walk back inside and have the smell delight me upon opening our front door.

As the concoction continues to simmer and bubble, it is time to cut flour and butter together, to stir in milk and press biscuits onto a baking sheet. The rise and browning smell in the oven will draw rumbly tummies in to wonder when it will be ready, and once-a-year apple butter will be served fresh and hot right from the Crockpot on buttery and flaky biscuits.

Layer upon layer rises together to create the perfect biscuit, and that sort of sums up the entire apple-picking adventure. It is all the layers working together beautifully. If any one of the above-mentioned layers was missing from our outing, we would have to adjust and learn a new rhythm, but for the moment, the comfort in the familiar is a gift we treasure. (And it sure doesn't hurt that it ends in something as delicious as warm apple butter on a fresh homemade biscuit right from the oven!)

Weight of Blankets

It is an unseasonably chilly night. I've tried to resist turning on the heat this week, but I finally cave and adjust the thermostat. I feel my entire self breathe a sigh of relief. I've got on warm clothes, fuzzy slippers, and have an old quilt thrown over my lap. Every time I move, the chill sweeps through me until I get settled in a warm spot again.

Getting ready to climb in bed, I realize that our lightweight quilt will not provide enough warmth for the cold, damp weather. There is an afghan on the chair in the corner, a chair we lovingly refer to as the "Peace Chair", so named for the days of restoring peace to our home with littles. The afghan – oatmeal-colored with green stripes – was my first crochet project.

In my single days, a friend offered to teach me to crochet, and of course, I decided that a full-size afghan would be a great inaugural project. I'm kind of surprised that I finished it and that it turned out, but it's lovely and I enjoy the weight and warmth it provides in cold snaps like this. Folded in half, it perfectly covers my side of the bed, so I get double the weight and warmth.

After crawling in bed, I realize I might need another blanket. My sock feet pad across the floor to the fireplace hearth, where a yellow wire basket sits just for the purpose of holding blankets. I grab a lovely vintage quilt gifted by a dear friend.

This quilt, passed down through her family, is the perfect softness that you think of in a worn and loved quilt. It was my faithful companion when I had pneumonia a couple of years ago – plopped on the couch or sitting outside for a few minutes every day, covered up in this quilt, resting, recovering, and healing. It, too, doubles and covers my side of the bed just right.

Our little beagle gets cold easily, and during seasons like this, he burrows under the covers to find a warm nest for the night (or during the day too!). There is something very cozy and comforting about finding a place to nest and rest.

Now under a bounty of layers, I can't help but express thanks and gratitude for the lovely feeling that it gives me to slide under the weight of the blankets. This is not the kind of weight that feels like a burden, but rather the weight that feels like a tight hug, a comfort, and a cocoon of warmth.

A Warm Welcome

Early one morning in my quiet time spot, snuggled under a cozy blanket, I was reading the final chapters in the book of Acts. I've read this before, but coming across the first ten verses in Acts 28 is always inspiring to me.

Paul and fellow travel-mates have been on a ship for longer than expected due to terrible weather. They finally make it to land, but only after a shipwreck, near-starvation, being stranded, and facing death. I absolutely love what happens when they get to land though.

Here is what we know about the scene: upon arrival, the travelers don't even know the name of where they are, only that it is cold and raining. The locals come out with a genuine welcome and build a warming and inviting fire.

I try to put myself in the shoes of the weary travelers and imagine how incredible this welcome would feel after the harrowing experiences they have just survived. What relief they must feel to have their feet on solid ground and find some of the comforts of home even in a new and strange place. The locals were open with their hospitality to those they did not know – and don't forget that a number of those who had arrived were prisoners.

While this fire kindled warmth, it likely also kindled a spark of hope that may have nearly or completely gone out in these who had faced death. And it strikes me that my hospitality may also be an opportunity to not only invite someone warmly into my life or a conversation but perhaps even from death to life.

This sounds like heavenly hospitality! Knowing that we have a future home God is preparing for us, we can seek opportunities to welcome others to join us. Revelation 3:20 gives us a similar homey picture of salvation: "Behold, I stand at the door and knock. If anyone hears my voice and opens the door, I will come in to him and eat with him, and he with me." Here we see the home of our hearts – what kind of welcome will the Lord receive there? Will it be warm and inviting? Or cold and sterile?

Once we have the Lord living inside our hearts, how will that pour out into our actions, conversations, and even our hospitality? If we continue reading in Acts 28, we see that the Maltans – those firebuilders on the shore – continued to show gracious care and kindness to their visitors and to provide generously for their guests.

When I see the word "hospitality" tonight, I see the word "hospital" in it. When we don't feel good, we need gentle and tender care, proper nourishment, and genuine love. Those who arrived on the rocky edges of land were in great need, and they received a warm welcome whose echo reverberates through the ages to inspire us in serving others as well.

We may never know what eternal impact may come from the selfless gift of a warm welcome. Smile at that stranger. Open your door. Engage in conversation. And, yes – build a warming fire if needed. Use the gift of friendship to kindle a spark of hope that may grow into a flame of faith burning for the Kingdom of Christ!

OLD Country FARM
ADORN
THE
DARK

An Ordinary Evening at Home

Plopped on the couch with a blanket over my lap, I marvel at the beautiful everydayness of a quiet evening at home. Stacks of books and papers are perched nearby on the coffee table, and shoes are strewn in various nooks and crannies.

The dishwasher hums, our dog wants someone to play with him, and there are alternating pockets of quiet and asking questions about the day that has passed or the day to come. Homework is pulled out of backpacks and perhaps a funny happening of the day is retold.

Music drifts in from another room and the clock ticks. Sock feet stretch out and prop up on the coffee table or are tucked up on the couch under a blanket. We look through the mail, read books, play games, and work puzzles.

Our dog barks and we wonder why, but sometimes not enough to investigate. There is news to read, a new day to plan, friends and family to communicate with. There are tests to study for, laundry to fold, missing shoes to find, and problems to solve. There are lunches to pack, coats to hang up, and questions to ponder.

It is so ordinary that we may even miss it, not realizing how nice it is to just be at home. An ordinary evening looks different for each of us in different seasons – boisterous, quiet, calm, or chaotic. Allowing ourselves to be comfortable with our ordinary is a gift. It is a sweet spirit of contentment. In these moments, we realize that everyone has laundry to do, and no one is exempt from junk mail or cleaning interesting looking things out of the fridge. This is where we find common ground sometimes, in putting on our comfy pants, propping sock feet on the coffee table, and just being ordinary.

Yellow Chair

At 5:30 am, the alarm sounds and wakes me from my peaceful slumber. Early-morning darkness and that extra quiet of no one else being awake greets me. I turn off the recording that I sleep to every night (a bubbling mountain creek from our favorite camping spot!) and put my retainer in the green plastic case. Slow, quiet steps lead me through the dark to the living room, where my thrifted yellow chair is tucked into a corner.

I close the hall door to keep sound to a minimum for sleeping teenagers, and click on the black industrial lamp that creates a soft and warm glow for my little corner. This is where I meet with the Lord each morning.

Reaching into the also-thrifted Longaberger basket, I draw out my floral journal and soft leather Bible. Leafing through the thin pages to get to the right spot, I tuck one foot up on the chair. Letting the words tumble through the air into my eyes, into my brain, into my heart, and then out through my pen, I process what I'm reading and prayerfully consider how to apply it. Time in prayer follows, and then a chapter or two of whatever faith-building book I'm currently reading.

The yellow chair is the perfect nesting spot. It is where I start the first hour of my day. At my left hand is a wire basket, gently holding a worn and cozy quilt for chilly mornings. At my feet is a needlepoint footstool passed down in our family. On my right, a basket of things I might want during this time.

I would love to know the story of this yellow chair. It was spotted in a thrift store one morning, and I talked myself out of it and left it there. By later in the day, I was telling one of my girls about it, and she agreed to go back to the shop and see if it was still there. It was, and we brought it home. To me, it is homey and cozy. It is vintage looking in a good way, and it is small and fits me better than the big, bulky furniture of our modern day. I love the gentle glide and the wooden accents on the arms.

It is perfectly accessorized with a simple pillow and small lap afghan that I crocheted a few years ago. The yellow chair is one of my perches. I frequently spend a Sunday afternoon here or curl up in the evening with a Bible study or a good book. And, yes, this is where I savor the first hour of most days.

This little corner of my world is safe. It is set apart – not so much physically, perhaps, but it definitely calls me to set myself apart mentally from the fray of the world. When I'm in the yellow chair, life is slower and I am calmer and at peace. No, there is nothing magical about an upholstered combination of wood and springs. Instead, it's the invitation the chair offers – to set myself apart and just be still – that makes each quiet moment enchanting.

The Imperfect Beauty and Shelter of Relationships

Frayed Edges

On a Colorado-cold December Thursday in 2018, I acquired a gray Broncos sweatshirt. I had wanted it for a while, even though I'm not a sports fan and am pretty useless at knowing which team is doing well in any given year. Sweatshirts are the epitome of cozy anyway and though this one is way too big and has frayed edges at the hem and cuffs, it's also the warmest thing in my closet, and I will never part with it.

The Broncos sweatshirt belonged to my dad during his time on earth, and the morning after he passed into heaven, it became mine. I wore it that day to think of him, to try to feel his warm hug and be closer to him in some way. That day, my mom and I cared for details, made endless phone calls, and were generally worn out – we were frayed around the edges, too.

We went to his favorite BBQ place for dinner that evening, ate brisket, and toasted our yellow plastic cups of soda: "here's to you Pepaw!" Diners around us carried on as though nothing had happened, though some of them carried burdens of their own that we didn't know about.

Three years later, I still think of my dad often and wish I could feel his arms around me once more. If you ever see me wearing a too-warm, too-big sweatshirt with blue lettering on it, I just might need an extra hug, frayed edges and all.

Miss Sue's Popcorn

It's just an ordinary Sunday evening in February. The sky is clear and crisp, allowing us to see the stars, the moon and nearly our breath. We watch the clock and count the minutes until it is time. Clothed in pajamas and slippers and wrapped in quilts, we dash across the street to Miss Sue's.

Miss Sue is our dear neighbor. She and her husband are like grandparents to us, and we love them so. They always greet us with a warm hug and smile, and we feel like family when we are at their house. As soon as we enter and get our hugs, we can already hear the *pop, pop, pop* in the microwave and smell the mouth-watering aroma of what we know is coming.

We trot across the street every Sunday evening during *When Calls the Heart* season, and we are invited into Miss Sue's family room, where we each choose a recliner or a section on the couch. Enveloped in the quilts we carried over, we make ourselves at home and grab a red plastic bowl for popcorn. News is traded back and forth – how has your week been, how is your family, what's new in your life as we munch on the warm kernels of corn that are perfectly salted.

My daughters have asked numerous times about what kind of popcorn it is and how we can make our own at home. We buy the exact same brand and variety she serves, but as one of my girls says, "Ours is never the same."

Opinions are swapped about the episode, and we turn the volume down during commercials to share more pieces of life and just enjoy being together. Some people are just easy to be with, you know? At the end, dishes are whisked away to the kitchen, blankets are wrapped around sleepy shoulders, and we give hugs and thank yous along with the promise to see each other again next Sunday.

Everything about this is such a delight to me. I've longed to have this kind of neighbor and to be this kind of neighbor. And it is not lost on me that this is a sweet gift and an uncommon grace. I wonder what our other neighbors think about us skipping across the street at night in our pajamas, beaming with expectation and joy? But I find that I don't care – it is an opportunity for us to slow down and find joy in simply spending time together.

All the way home, we exclaim to one another about what fun we had and how much we love Miss Sue. I think there is something in each of our hearts that feels fed and refreshed by the calm and the peace of these one-hour jaunts. There are other sweet memories of her in our mental scrapbooks as well, such as the time I made stacks of waffles and we compiled what we had for "breakfast for dinner" and played games during a hurricane watch. There were evenings snuggling up to watch Christmas movies, and even the time we shared an Easter dinner together.

Someday maybe I will have the joy of being this kind of neighbor to another family in our neighborhood, but for now, we are happy recipients of Miss Sue's popcorn, friendship, and a sweet welcome into her life, which brings all the cozy feelings to our hearts.

Porch Swing

Still-growing bare feet stepped out onto the front porch in mid-January. A gasp of delight greeted my ears as my fourteen-year-old-daughter exclaimed over what a beautiful day it was and beckoned me to join her. Still wearing my slippers and feeling thankful for her appreciation of the beauty of an unexpectedly warm afternoon, I was happy to oblige.

We sat next to each other on the porch swing that had been there since we bought the house 17 years ago. The owner came back after we had closed and asked for the swing back, but I couldn't let it go. It has been a place of rest and solitude to us, inviting a slowing down that we so appreciate.

After chillier-than-usual days in the South, the warmth of the sun was like putting on a sweater fresh from the dryer. It was the kind of heat that seeps into your soul and warms the spirit as well as the body. Errands were waiting, but we had to be home for an expected service call, so the afternoon stretched before us without anything of consequence needing our attention. We lingered deliciously, watching a yellow butterfly flounce through the air, hearing the birds, and noticing the jet stream in the sky.

Scout, our beagle, joined us outside for a nap in the sun. After lazing about in the grass, he curled up between us on the porch swing while we slowly swayed back and forth. We talked about everything and nothing, and all that really mattered was being in the moment. As the minutes ticked into an hour, the spaciousness of slowing down felt like an unexpected grace I hadn't known I needed.

*

Today, it is gray and drippy and cozy. My diffuser is running with the spicy scent of cinnamon and cloves, the tap of raindrops is hitting the skylights, a candle is flickering, and there is a sense of calm permeating our home. I'm pulling back from the world and enjoying the simple joy of being home, and the deep breath that gives a needed pause.

Just now, a bird is singing outside my window. Perhaps it is delighted in the rain and the hope of the worms that will be found after it finishes. Somehow, that little bird is finding joy in being alive today. The lamplight inside our living room glows brighter when it is gray outside, and I find the warmth of glowing light compelling and inviting.

On days like this, two simple words – everything and nothing – sway back and forth in my mind like a porch swing, humming a gentle rhythm of grace.

The Mommy Touch

I recently bought a new robe. Not just any robe – I would call it more of a cozy wrap. The tag inside says "Cozy All Day," and I'm here for it. The super soft, oversized, pale pink cocoon is just the epitome of coziness.

This whole experience brought me immediately back to my childhood, where my mama was adorned in a blue chenille robe. It zipped up the front and had pockets on the sides. I'm not sure how it started, but I specifically remember that her robe had – as I called it – the "Mommy Touch."

You know what I mean by this, right? The perfect texture of comfort and cozy, so soft it felt like home and peace. It was familiar and inviting, safe and warm. I've been trying to describe it to my own children, and though words somehow fail, I can still conjure up the imagery in my memories.

I think that robe was a symbol of all the things my mom stood for to me. Even then, I realized the power and beauty of home, love, comfort, and acceptance. A sweet friend of mine calls this "a soft place to land" and that is exactly what we mothers try to offer to our families.

The world is harsh – the Mommy Touch is soft.

The world tries to get us to conform – the Mommy Touch accepts.

The world is cold and uninviting – the Mommy Touch is warm and inviting.

The world can fill us with anxiety – the Mommy Touch brings peace.

The world is dangerous – the Mommy Touch is safe.

The world is foreign sometimes – the Mommy Touch is familiar.

The world is mean and hateful – the Mommy Touch is loving and kind.

God shows such deep kindness, and one of the kindnesses He has shown me is a 1980s blue chenille robe and the memory of the Mommy Touch.

Let's Talk about Our Day

A pallet of sleeping bags and quilts on the floor of my childhood room would be waiting for my son Samuel when we arrived at my parents' house. Pastel green and mauve wallpaper that I picked out for my 16th birthday is smoothed over the lower half of the wall, and a coordinating border outlines the ceiling.

This cozy little spot became his over the years of visits and being the youngest. He took over the space like a boss, stashing things under the bed, adding his own beloved western-themed baby quilt, and always keeping a few toys or books nearby.

Many nights, as I would be in the process of tucking him in, my dad would come down the hallway and say in his rich, deep voice, "Samuel, want to talk about our day?" With the lights low, man and boy would gently chat about the events of the day. Most likely they both already knew all the things the other would say, having spent the day in one another's company, but there was a cadence and rhythm to discussing it together before submitting to a quiet night of rest.

There might be a low chuckle or an outright cackle (depending on who was laughing) at something funny the other said. There might be a tender moment over a sweet memory or perhaps a hard spot in the day. The rest of us could hear the low murmur of their nightly ritual, a simple practice some might have thought was nothing. Instead, it was everything.

Now that my dad is in heaven, Samuel has mentioned missing this tradition. Knowing that he could tell Pepaw about his day and vice versa was a calming lullaby for him, and a beautiful gift for this grateful mama who listened to them talk about their days from the shadows in the dark hallway.

Tables

Chairs pull up to the edges, where elbows rest. Hands are grasped around as we bow for prayer. How many conversations have happened around the four sides of this table? How many loved ones have gathered here? How many meals have been served?

Our table came from the "bargain dinette" section of a secondhand furniture store. A maple drop leaf with six chairs, its shape and design captivated me. The finish had seen better days, but that became my project over the next few summers as I sanded, stripped, and refinished every bit of it. I've now done it twice, and the table continues to serve us with grace and strength.

Strangers have been served at our table, as well as dear friends and both of our dads (my husband's and mine, who are now in heaven, feasting at the table of the Lamb). The number of meals served at our table is inching toward 20,000. Some of them were fancy and took a lot of effort, and others were takeout meals after barely surviving that day. But the privilege was always there – the chance to nurture souls and cultivate relationships with those who gathered around our table.

We bump elbows and crack corny jokes, causing eye-rolls as we are just plain silly together. But we also talk about what we heard at church, how school went, and who we can be praying for. The table is a place of offering, an altar of sorts where we lay out a meal as an act of worship to the dear One who provided every morsel, the energy to prepare it, and the rhythm of partaking together. (If you want to explore this idea further, I've written much more about tables in my book *Beauty Maker*!)

Today I see crumbs and sticky places that were missed in the cleaning up. I see scuff marks from where my chair rubs against the table leg, and smears from hands wiped on the seat cushion. Today I see papers that need to be put away, stray napkins left behind, and cups that didn't make it to the dishwasher. But when I close my eyes and think about what really matters, I see thousands of moments spent together around this very table. Doing art projects, carving pumpkins, decorating cookies, and yes, enjoying meals. Drawing friends in and pulling up more chairs. Creating beauty and community, a place of worship and beauty in the seemingly ordinary and mundane.

As we scrape plates across the surface and chaos abounds, the table stands tall, quietly serving those who pull their chairs up to the edge.

Every hour I need thee

Creating an Inviting Atmosphere

In years past, I described one of my favorite things to do as setting a pretty table and inviting others to join me for the joy, delight, and beauty of the experience. Upon thinking about it further, I've realized that what I really love is creating an inviting atmosphere.

It is a place where friends and family come and feel welcome, feel free to be themselves – to kick their shoes off and put their feet on our coffee table. To open cabinets to find what they need and feel at home. To ask for something that would help them be more comfortable and to know that I want to provide anything they need!

Creating an inviting atmosphere is about more than just the outward appearance. It's about creating a place where others feel accepted and wanted, a place where God will be at work in the heart as well. An inviting atmosphere is something that appeals to the senses in order to put a restless heart at ease, calm an anxious mind and body, and meet basic needs while reducing distractions. When those things are out of the way, there is more space and room for the Holy Spirit to be at work!

Yes, this can be done on a larger scale by serving in the local church or at an event, but I think a very powerful way it can be lived out is right in our own homes. What would be needed for you to feel that you are in an inviting atmosphere? How can you practice serving those around you with some of those things in order to allow a spacious place for the Spirit of God to be at work?

I've mentioned this before, but we can also pray for the obedience to create an inviting atmosphere in our very own hearts for our dear Savior to come in and make His dwelling right inside of us. What a joy that is for both of us when He has a warm welcome and a place prepared in our hearts to do His work and take up residence in love.

Summer Evening

A red, white, and blue tablecloth covers the wood picnic table stained red and standing firm on the cement patio at my parents' house. The nearby crabapple tree is laden with fruit, and the squirrels chatter and scurry to and fro. Daisies are trimmed from the flower beds in front and gathered into a pitcher to adorn the table.

The nearby grill is fired up, and hamburgers and hotdogs are made ready for their turn over the heat. A Tupperware tray holds the meat that is splashed with Lawry's salt and Worcestershire sauce.

Meanwhile, beans bubble on the stove and brownies bake in the oven. Creamy vanilla custard is spinning in the ice cream maker parked on the back stoop. A wet spot begins to form on the cement as ice and salt are added at regular intervals. The silver canister is popped into the freezer when it has reached completion.

It has been a few years since I've had a hamburger grilled by my dad, and it is one of the things I will always miss about him. There was just something perfect about a burger grilled by him in my parents' Colorado backyard.

Dad would whistle and sing while standing watch at the grill. He'd pop his head in the screen door and give a five-minute warning for us to finish up the rest of the food. And then he would bring his offering to the table – a platter of burgers and hot dogs grilled just the way he always did them. I don't know how else to describe them, other than to say they were his signature – charred just right on the outside, and moist and juicy on the inside.

After dinner, we might pull out the croquet game or reach for a book to be read aloud. We would eat brownies and ice cream and linger longer with nothing else really calling our attention. My kids loved Pepaw's grass. The lush, thick carpet of green he accomplished in the desert climate of Colorado was truly a marvel. He was extremely proud of it, and rightfully so. The kids would lie down in it and watch the clouds, pointing out shapes and playing guessing games.

We still do many of these things, and though it isn't really the same without dad there, the magic of memories still holds us captive. These long, slow, wonderful summer evenings hold a certain appeal and sweet spot in my mind and heart. There are so many things I'd want to do with one extra day with him, but a Dad-grilled burger would definitely make the list!

Missing Dad's Voice

December marks the anniversary of my dad's passing. In year three, I find myself missing his voice and fearing that I might not be able to conjure it up in my mind one day.

My mom and I are doing a puzzle in our living room near the glow of the Christmas tree, and I pull out my phone and turn on some Christmas music. The Oak Ridge Boys is the music of my childhood, and one of the voices sounds very similar to my dad. Oh, how I wish I could hear him sing along again!

A week later, I remember a recorded Hallmark storybook in my closet that has Dad's voice recorded in it. I pull it out and open the cover, but nothing happens. The plastic battery box is full of corroded batteries, and I am upset that I let this happen by storing the book with the batteries in it.

New batteries are tried. Lots of corrosion is cleaned and wiped and swiped out. A couple of You-Tube videos and lots of frustration later, I am about to give up when my husband gets it to work. The tears spring to my eyes at the first sound of the deep cadence of Dad's voice. I haven't heard it in three years. There I stand in my closet, getting ready for the Christmas Eve service, listening to dad's voice roll over my ears and sink deep into my heart. This feels like a Christmas miracle, and I keep it tucked away for after church to bring out and surprise everyone – especially my mom.

Of course, hearing his voice again on any day of the year would bring tears to our eyes, but what a gift to have him be part of our Christmas Eve tradition once again, and in such an unexpected way.

The Comfy Test

Taking little boys shopping is not for the faint of heart – can I get an amen?! When my son was little, he would be plopped in a shopping cart and not super thrilled with his lot in life. One thing that got us through many a visit to a store was to find an empty hanger – he would spend the whole time making it into a weapon and making all the accompanying sound effects. Bless. I will just apologize now to anyone he ever pointed it at, but it was my saving grace in those days.

Anyway, as we patrolled the store, he invented what he called the "Comfy Test": whenever I would pick out something I wanted to purchase or even try on, he would rub it on his cheek. This was to determine if it passed his standards of being comfy.

Was it soft when he rubbed it on his cheek? Was it scratchy? I don't know if he wondered how it would feel when I hugged him or what, because frequently these clothing items were not for him – but he was fiercely committed to his method, and he would let me know if the item was approved.

Now that he is a teenager, the official Comfy Test doesn't really happen anymore. Yes, I still love soft, comfy, clothes but somehow it's not the same as having my little boy insert his opinion about the fabrics and materials.

However, his method still speaks to me about how we come across to others – are we prickly and off-putting, or soft and inviting? Are others comfortable around us? Do they want to draw close to us (and, by extension, to God)?

In other words, do our words and actions pass the Comfy Test?

Strawberry Picking

Most years in the spring, we are eager to head to the local berry patch to select red, juicy, jewel-like berries from the rows of plants. We've taken friends, picnics, gone alone – but we try to always go and remember the simplicity and joy of picking berries. God's creativity abounds in food, and I hope our enjoyment of His gift of berries rises like the laughter of children experiencing joy at this treat.

Berries warmed by the overhead sun are picked and bitten into right there in the rows – juice dribbling down chins and charming me with the delight of childhood as my mind takes a snapshot to treasure. Picking them is only the first of the joys – we know we will slice them and serve them alongside dinner on the screened-in porch, and make jam and strawberry shortcake for dessert.

When my girls were little, I felt ambitious one day and made jam around lunch time. One child was in a highchair, and the other was at the table with something to nibble on. I must've forgotten how jam doubles in size when bubbling over the heat, and my pan was too small, so the whole batch bubbled over, steamed, smoked, and generally made a sticky mess.

About this time, a lady from our church came over and immediately stepped in to help – the door was open to let out smoke, the girls were watching in puzzlement, and I was embarrassed. We all lived through it, though, and a gem came from this a few days later, when one of our neighbors was burning leaves in their backyard. Our oldest daughter lifted her eyes to the smoke between the trees and said, "They must be making jam too, Mama!" HA!

With no toddling legs in our house anymore and more careful remembrance about the doubling of the boiling liquid that becomes jam, we haven't had any repeats of this experience. But somehow, even though it felt overwhelming at the time, I now find myself smiling at the simple sweetness of seeing it all through young, tender eyes.

Then I pull out the food processor and pour in almonds and butter and cornmeal. Simple muffin scones are prepared to slice in half and layer with berries and mounds of freshly whipped cream. The colors and flavors layered together are made more of a celebration simply by the fact that we don't have it very often – its rarity is part of the gift.

Berries are piled atop morning pancakes, packed in lunches, and added to smoothies. It's just a little thing, but over and over through the years, when we go back to the same farm, I see little legs toddling through the rows. I remember carrying one child in the wrap while chasing two others, recall teaching little fingers how to pick only the largest and reddest berries and leave the blossoms and green berries to mature and ripen.

It strikes my mind just now that my babies were like those little blossoms when I first took them to the berry patch. Now all three teenagers, and they are ripening and maturing into lovely treasures provided by God. May they bring sweetness to those around them and add delight to the lives they touch!

Childhood Sick Days

Huddled on the couch watching life move by without me.

Watching my family at dinner while I just doze off and on.

My mom bringing me cauliflower cheese soup and garlic bread from an iconic pizza place that was part of my growing up years.

Trying to watch *Pollyanna* while I was in and out of sleep.

Sipping Lipton's Noodle Soup and Bigelow Plantation Mint tea.

Slouching around in my pj's all day, no better place to be than home.

Friends or family calling to check on how I'm feeling – a connection to the world I felt disconnected from.

Sipping 7-Up through a straw and nibbling on saltines.

Laying on a pallet on the floor next to the heat vent and listening to a record recounting the story of Clara Barton.

Everything looking so different from my little nest on the floor – dad was taller, the windows were higher and I was smaller.

I'm not trying to minimize the misery of sick days, but these are the cozy thoughts that come to mind in the midst of remembering sick days from my own childhood. Truthfully, mercy is not a strength of mine, and I tend to stress when I know someone in my home is sick, thinking of all the what-ifs, the details to rearrange, and the fear of it spreading through the whole house. And all of this was pre-pandemic!

My point is this: in times of sickness or other weaknesses, what I remember is not the illness or how long it lasted, but the love and care I received in the midst of it. These are the cozy memories of sick days that comfort and warm my heart years later, and this challenges me to be more intentional about providing this kind of love and care to those around me who aren't feeling well!

Fun Team

In my early-to mid-twenties, I worked at a charming retreat center. As with any job there were some challenges to overcome as we experienced a sudden transition in leadership. Offices were switched around, and there was a hushed tone of uncertainty as change abounded.

Not long after this, a group of three guys – who also worked there – declared themselves the Fun Team. They visited a local thrift store and bought Mr. Rogers-era cardigans, got some sort of instant camera, and took it upon themselves to introduce fun back into our workplace.

I received an invite from the Fun Team to go out to lunch one work day, and I don't remember a thing about where we went or what we did except the impression of these three cardigan-wearing, smiling faces approaching my desk and snapping a quick photo for remembrance. I wish I knew where that photo was.

You may be wondering how this fits in to a cozy lifestyle. Well, here is my take on it – cozy is the art of helping myself and others feel welcome, wanted, at home, and at rest. Inviting others in to my life or being intentional to engage with them in some way is a way of showing that warm welcome and inviting anxious hearts to rest.

Life is not always fun and rarely easy, but maybe we could put a smile on someone else's face by declaring ourselves the Fun Team for a day. I bet it will make your heart smile, too!

SHATTO
MILK COMPANY
FAMILY

Picnics

I've long thought that food tastes better outside. There is just something delightful about breathing in the fresh air and hearing the birds chirp nearby with the canopy of sky overhead to spark imagination and enjoyment.

Laying a sheet or cloth over a picnic table or simply spreading a quilt on the ground softens the view and lends an inviting air. Whether you choose paper plates or enamel speckled picnic dishes, the outcome is the same: delight. Whether you choose paper napkins, cloth, or even spare bandanas, the outcome is the same: memorable. No matter what you choose to serve, the outcome is the same: nourishing.

You may find a pinecone or a sprig of something blooming to lay across the center of your table, or bring a small cup or jar and a pair of scissors to create a sweet centerpiece. It is a palette for the beauty maker to create a lovely table scene and invite others with her to gather around the table and enjoy a meal.

One year for my birthday, the only thing I wanted was to have a picnic for each meal. We started with a sunrise picnic of cinnamon rolls served on a quilt at one of the local boat landings. The sky was beautiful, and we'll never forget how a boat came along and the wake caused the floating dock we were sitting on to lurch, followed by our laughter at nearly losing our balance and pan of breakfast! For lunch, we went through a drive-thru, and in our new-normal pandemic world, we had a picnic in the car, feasting on chicken sandwiches and salty fries. Dinner was take-out pizzas at the waterfront park on a weathered wooden table with an ice cream dessert waiting nearby in the cooler.

We've had picnics at the beach, in the mountains, in the woods, and at home on our driveway. No day is too ordinary for a picnic, and it instantly elevates the meal to a new level! A breakfast picnic of waffles and berries served in the courtyard of the apartments I was living in, Fourth of July picnics at a historic site with my mom where we munched on chicken salad, muffins, and brownies, or a Christmas hot cocoa bar outside – each is a treasured memory. One time I served breakfast in a rose garden where I was working, and another time a fellow co-worker invited me to share grilled cheese and tomato soup on a quilt over our lunch break.

Pancake picnics on our driveway were a treat when my children were young and Daddy had to work late. We've had picnics on our coffee table, on the floor in front of the fireplace, in parks, and in hotel rooms. A picnic brings a bit of home on the road – something familiar to perhaps unfamiliar surroundings.

Picnics bring us together, but I also think they slow us down. How often do we sit at our dining room table, eat, and get right back up and go on with our individual things? When we are on a picnic, we might be more prone to linger, go for a walk, pick wildflowers, marvel at the bubbling of the creek nearby, or watch a bird. Our kids may climb on rocks, run through the grass, or stare at the clouds and see what shapes are hiding there.

May I invite you to think about how to add picnics to your life? Whether you plan an elaborate spread at a local park or carry paper plates into the backyard, you may be surprised by how the slow, sweet gift of dining under the open sky nourishes your heart.

S L O W D

Everyday Magic of Simple Pleasures

Enamelware

Lightweight pots and pans of tin
Perfect to carry your picnic in.
Painted in shades of red, white, and blue
Striped on the edge or speckled too.
They are humble, hard-working
Long-lasting and charming.
Telling a story of simpler days
Now cast aside for new-fashioned ways.

They welcome us to slow life down
To go outside and look around.
To open our eyes to what God has made
We quiet ourselves in the sun or the shade.
Sipping a mug of something hot
Hurrying and busy are the things we are not.
To newer and bigger and more, we say no
Choosing instead the quiet way to go.

Lord, make me a vessel able as this
Inviting others to a sweet place of rest.
Where creeks bubble, birds sing, and trees sway in the breeze
Casting cares upon You brings our hearts ease.
Let me be humble, versatile, and kind
Not worrying if I'm the one left behind
But seeking to serve You in all that I do
And looking for ways to bring glory to You.

The Ministry of Soup

Cutting two celery ribs and bright carrots into chunks, peeling the paper-thin layers of skin from a head of savory garlic, snipping sprigs of rosemary from the garden, dicing an onion, and adding spices and water – these simple motions create a rhythm of peace that brings a sense of calm and almost holiness to the task of making dinner.

Wisps of steam rise from the Dutch oven simmering on the stove. The aromas of meat, vegetables, broth, and seasonings meld together and waft through the house, beckoning us to take a deep breath, to slow down and pause. We look forward with anticipation of the meal to come.

As the days grow cool and dark, I start thinking of favorite soup recipes. Lighting a candle, stirring together a favorite recipe, or enjoying the creativity of trying something new. Wrapping my hands around the warmth of the bowl and enjoying the gift of soup with all of my senses, it is like a liquid hug I can gift myself or someone around me.

Soup makes me think of simpler and slower times. I see spiritual parallels abounding as I think about the act and picture of making soup. It speaks to me of flavor, fragrance, and nourishment.

Your Special Flavor

Soup is so much more than a pot of hot water. It invites intricate flavor profiles and the synergy of combined ingredients. Each element is needed and welcome. A soup of potatoes and water would be decidedly uninviting. It needs herbs, salt, and broth for starters. It is a great example of teamwork rather than a solo performance! This is the time to come together and shine when blended with other unique ingredients.

On a hard day when nothing seems to be going right, tossing a few mismatched and maybe even shriveled ingredients into a pot of water can become a work of art. Even when we feel cast aside and like we aren't worth much, we can still be useful to flavoring a piece of beauty for God's kingdom!

Consider how a carrot can only contribute the properties and flavor of carrots. It can never impart the taste of an onion or the earthiness of thyme. As people, we are the same. Each of us has a unique contribution to make to the Kingdom of God. We can only contribute what we have to offer and must not become stuck in a web of comparison and discouragement that we aren't able to contribute different things. The soup is not complete without each ingredient, just as the body of Christ is not complete without our special offering. How does the unique way God has equipped you contribute flavor to the community of believers around you?

The Fragrance of Grace

Soup making is ministry because it slows down our own hearts and allows us to consider that even as the fragrance of the bubbling stew fills our home in a peaceful way, so our prayers and praises rise as a pleasing aroma to the very throne of God.

The wafting fragrance of soup in our homes is something that draws others in and makes our tummies growl at the thought of the delicious soup attached to the smell we are experiencing. Imagine the Gospel in and through our lives being so compelling!

Consider that we have been through a long couple of years where we may have felt peeled bare, chopped up, and thrown into a pot of hot water – but can we say that nourishing things have come out of us in the midst of this? Have we learned new things or chosen joy in the midst of struggle? Just as soup ingredients offer nutrition that feeds our soul and bodies, we can choose to bring life and health to those around us when we respond to hardship with grace.

The fragrance of grace is the permeating aroma of God's presence in our lives that overflows into conversation, interaction with each other, and the way we care for one another. The number one way to increase our fragrance for the Father is to spend time with Him. How are you doing in prioritizing your time with the Lord?

Nourishing Service

Soup delivers nourishment on a variety of levels. It speaks to our senses, satisfies our hunger, and brings health to our bodies. It is warming, comforting, and soothing.

It is a way of serving, a way of offering both love and ourselves in a life-giving way to those around us. It is ministry because we can allow ourselves to be taught through the ordinary act of celebrating God's provision through resources and time.

Delivering a jar of soup to a friend when they are sick is an act of comfort and love.

Laying out bowls, warming crusty bread, and pulling up our chairs to the table all create a feeling of invitation and expectance. We ladle out the hot soup, serving family members and friends alike; soup always seems to stretch and be enough for those around our tables. We give thanks for the simple ingredients that we are able to share.

Simmering on Truth

Soup seems almost magical in nature, combining little bits of this and that to create a delicious concoction that we will wonder how to replicate next time. It is taking what seems meager and watching it stretch, grow, and become something new and wonderful. The warmth and flavor of the broth is comforting and nourishing as we take that first sip and feel it warm our insides and satisfy our rumbling tummies.

We can find ministry in the mundane when we are looking *for* God and when we are looking *to* God. It sounds simple because it is. The next time you make soup, maybe you will consider your contribution to the body of Christ, the aroma that your life brings to His kingdom, and how you serve others with simple and nourishing actions.

NOURISH

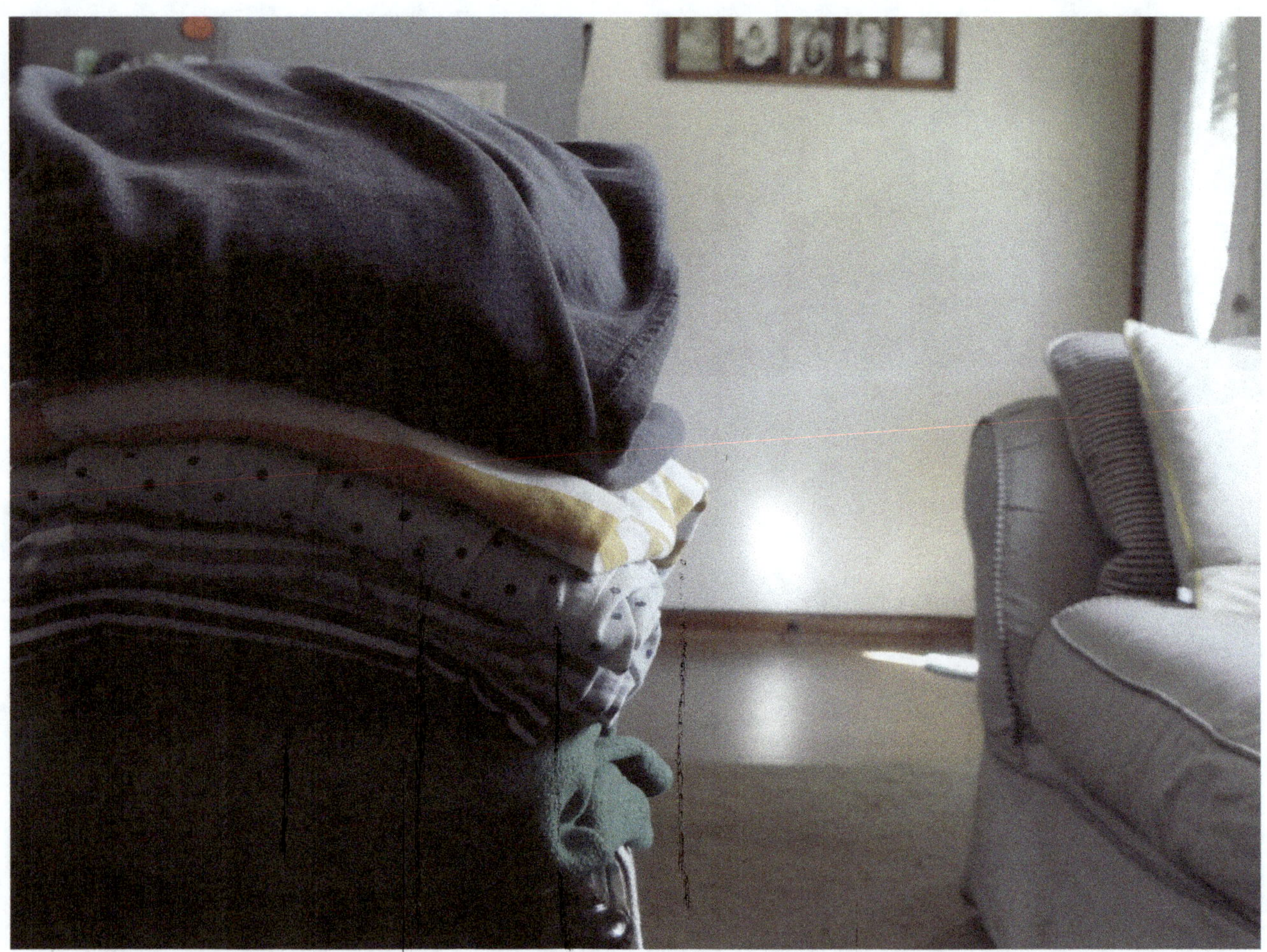

Warm Laundry

Hearing the dryer kick off from the other room, I grab a laundry basket and head that way. The warmth of the freshly dried clothes wisps out as I open the door. Piling socks and jammies and dishtowels in the blue basket with flowers printed on the bottom, I heft it up to my hip and make my way to the couch. I want to pour the whole basket over my lap and just sit with the warmth for a minute.

I want to appreciate the gift that we have access to so much convenience when doing laundry. Yes, it never ends; yes, it gets left all over the house. But can we just take a moment to appreciate that we have clean running water that swirls into the washer, and electricity that spins the drum and wrings all the clothes out when finished. After that, we simply have to move the clothes from one cylinder to the other, and pretty soon we have a basket full of clean and dry laundry to bless our families.

The clothes cool off all too fast, it seems, but while the warmth radiates, my folds move slower as I drape a towel over my lap and hands and sit for a moment. I slide my hand inside a sock to turn it right side out and may just leave my hand in there for a while as it cocoons me in warmth.

If you want an extra treat for yourself or a loved one on a cold day, stick a blanket or their pajamas in the dryer and surprise them with an extra cozy gift. Putting something on fresh from the dryer feels like receiving a hug, and it is so lovely.

A Fluffy Scarf

For the first time ever, I recently bought a fluffy scarf. Yes, I have a winter scarf but it is neither thick nor fluffy. It's cute – but definitely more for fashion than warmth. The chunky new scarf is a marvel and I wonder how I've never had one this warm before. It is homey and warm and thick and comfy. There is the coziest feeling wearing it – like draping a blanket around my neck and shoulders and calling it fashion.

Made of white yarn with stitches of gray sprinkled throughout, the long and cozy scarf is inviting to me. It is perfect when I get home from work and it feels cool in the house, but I don't really need a sweater. When looping the scarf around my neck, the woven layers begin to hold in warmth and bring a feeling of being wrapped in softness.

I wear it on a sunny day to walk Scout, our dog, and I wonder how many neighbors will laugh at me when I look ready for the Arctic because of its fluffiness, yet in reality it isn't even below 50 degrees outside! Who cares what they think! I'm comfortable and just the right temp, and this scarf is making me feel happy, so I toss aside the what-ifs like the long ends of the scarf tossed over my shoulder.

It's also perfect before bed and when I first get up in the morning and need an extra layer. My daughter says it's an excuse to wear a blanket, and I'm not disagreeing with her. I may be inexperienced at scarf wearing, but I'm already a huge fan and champion of big, fluffy, oversized scarves that are the epitome of cozy. Perhaps sometimes, a wearable blanket is just the kind of warm embrace we need!

Waiting for the Lids to Pop

Enamelware pot on the stove.

Waiting for water to boil.

Jars lined up, waiting their turn.

Lids placed on top and rings screwed on.

The sound of the water changes.

Reaching a full rolling boil.

Gently placing the jars inside.

Lid goes on top, timer is set.

A rack ready for the hot jars.

Carefully lifting them out.

Wait for it, wait for it – oh, the suspense!

Pop. Click. Ting.

It brings a smile to my face.

To hear each lid snap as it seals.

It's a song of the season – a true melody.

A homemaker's symphony serving her family.

Jars lined up in the cupboard.

Ready to adorn any meal.

Preserving the tastes of the season.

Until they come round next year.

Pulling out the canner again.

And waiting for the lids to pop.

THERMOS

Smiling about Thermoses

What is it that intrigues me about vintage thermoses and coolers? I can't stop loving them – and there are so many great varieties! Consider the evidence:

Thermos-brand personal thermoses can be found in varying sizes and shapes, like the quintessential red and black plaid that I took hot water in one year when my parents and I went to cut down a Christmas tree. I tried to make coffee for my dad afterward with some instant granules, and it was more like espresso! We've laughed about it for years. I had two of those thermoses and sent one to work with my husband, David, one chilly night when he had to work late. I thought I'd be all cute and put hot chocolate in it, and it never came home. Since then, a friend found another one in her mom's garage and instantly cried, "I know who would love this!" She brought it to me, and I felt so known!

The plaid of harvest browns and oranges makes perfect vessels for flowers on a fall table. Green with white stripes is perfect for casting a holiday mood when filled with evergreen sprigs. Then there's the navy blue one with a geometric pattern that I tried to leave at the thrift store – even though it was only $1 – because I was embarrassed to buy yet *another* thermos. (I went back for it.) I also love the silver one that David bought me on vacation in Michigan at an antique store one summer. Oh, and we bought one for our girls' room – so they are in on it now, too!

Then there are the foam coolers – short, squatty, and very round. I have a silver one that I've used for our water jug when we are camping and to display big blue hydrangea blooms on the Fourth of July. The red one has served the same purposes, and more recently, I found a green one. I am dreaming of using the red, green, and silver all together at Christmas.

In addition, there is an old silver rectangular cooler with an upper tray that holds things up out of the bottom. This was the first one I had, I think, and it was from a French flea market in Denver that my mom and I went to one Saturday. Despite its propensity to leak, I have enjoyed using this cooler for drinks at outdoor parties.

What could it possibly be that draws me to these campy, retro items? I do actually use them, but I also simply love how they look. They are charming, and come on, say it with me: they just don't make things like they used to!

I can now officially say that I have a thermos collection – I can't seem to stop! They just make me smile! I've taken pictures of them, used them in decorating, loaned them out, and even drawn some of them in permanent marker on a dishtowel.

Sure, I could sit here and come up with spiritual analogies for these thermoses – be hot or cold, not lukewarm! Store up for yourselves treasures in heaven where moth and rust do not destroy!

But I could also just as rightly say that these are just a little pleasure that I enjoy. I guess I don't have to know why I love thermoses! As any parent would, I believe that God delights in my delight over the colors and patterns in these little thermoses. They are nothing eternal, nothing supernatural – they just bring me joy, and that delights my Heavenly Father and causes me to delight in Him. Instead of feeling obsessed, I feel inspired. Instead of feeling stingy, I want to share. Instead of feeling greedy, I feel grateful. These are some of the gifts of thrifted thermoses.

CAMP COZY

Free Fruit

On an afternoon walk in December around our neighborhood, I spotted one of our neighbors sitting on a chair in his garage smoking a pipe. Wanting to stop by and check on him, I strode up the driveway. He didn't have his hearing aid in, so he had trouble hearing me as I asked how he and his wife were doing. His weathered and leathered skin framed his toothless gums.

As in years past, he quickly invited us to grab a bag and pick as many lemons, oranges, and tangerines as we wanted. The branches were bent heavy with harvest. Not having grown up in the south, it still seems a marvel and mystery to me to have living things so prolific in the winter.

And so, after crunching through leaves on our walk, we twisted orbs of yellow, gold, and orange to release their reliance on the tree and provide a new kind of beauty. The littlest oranges yielded their skin so easily that we accepted the invitation and divided sections among us right there underneath the branches, allowing the juice and sweetness to delight our tongues. Grocery bags were balanced on bike handlebars as we carried home our treasures and felt rich with the bounty we had been gifted.

Home for mere minutes, I had already sliced several oranges onto cookie sheets for drying, and we began our annual process of halving, squeezing, straining, and marveling over canning jars of lemon juice ready to be frozen in cubes to be used throughout the months ahead. One of my daughters grabbed a pretty basket, arranged her treasure, and skipped outside to take pictures of the mounds of beauty.

The bright, fresh scent explodes our senses and fills our home as we slice into globe after globe of fruit. We imagine all the ways we could make good use of this gift, who we can share a few with, and what generous provision we have been given. I remember last year when my sister and nieces were here at citrus-picking time and they participated with us. Then there was the year I made little tags and used the fruit as place cards for our holiday meal, propped up in cute ice cream dishes.

Over the months to come, we will drop a cube of lemon juice in hot tea, string up dried oranges, and simmer rinds on the stove. These are just small things, but each is a reminder to appreciate and enjoy the little gifts in life: simple, homey, pure ways to care for our homes and families. These feel like worship because they are, in a way, appreciating beauty and expressing thanks back to our Creator.

Noticing Small

In a world that embraces bigger and better, we can find simplicity and contentment in not only being noticers of small, but also cultivators and enjoyers of small blessings. Spring brings a unique opportunity for us to notice small things – a bare branch suddenly has tiny buds which bring delight and hope, little triangles of green poke their heads through the crumbly dirt at our feet and encourage us that new things are coming. Life is continuing, and growth is visible before our eyes.

Noticing the small allows us to practice contentment and delight in simple, everyday blessings and to consider how something small inside of us can grow and blossom as well. The green shoots bring hope, evoking juicy watermelons with sticky juice dripping down our chins as well as big balls of hydrangea blooms which will adorn our bushes and fill canning jars with bouquets throughout the early summer. We think of pies and crisps and sauces that will come from the humble yet versatile apple tree, and golden orbs which will season our pies and baking as well as cheer our porches with pumpkins in the season ahead.

Embracing small is valuable in life too – Kathleen Kelly (played by Meg Ryan) in *You've Got Mail* says, "Sometimes I wonder about my life. I lead a small life – well, valuable, but small – and sometimes I wonder, do I do it because I like it, or because I haven't been brave?" She ponders whether she has chosen small or whether she is hiding behind it. In our media- and fame-driven society, choosing small is certainly a brave choice. It is brave because it shows confidence in who we are without having to receive that approval from others.

The tender shoots that bravely push their heads up to the sun do so whether we notice or not. The trees put forth leaves without our applause. What would it look like for us to live like these small things? Doing what we were made to do without fear, pressure, or striving for acceptance? The butterfly confidently flutters around our yard, bringing beauty and a smile to our faces; so, too, can we be confident in embracing small and simple joys. These blessings are visible not only in nature but also in human nature, in our homes and even in ordinary, daily routines.

Practice being a noticer of small and make a list of the tiny things that bring joy, delight and contentment. Here are a few things to get you started:

- A lady bug by the front door.

- A colored leaf spotted on a morning walk.

- The song of a hummingbird speeding by.

- The fresh, new green of spring shoots emerging.

- Sun shining through the house as evening arrives or in the freshness of morning.

- Colorful butterflies floating through the yard.

- Whispers of sun rays filtering through the trees.

- Sitting on the front porch for no special reason.

- A wisp of steam rising from a mug of hot tea.

- The smell of something baking in the oven.

- Comfort from a cozy pair of socks.

Toast and Tea

When you're under the weather
Wishing to feel better
Toast and Tea

When you need something cozy
To make your outlook more rosy
Toast and Tea

The scent feels like home
The taste like a hug
Toast and Tea

So humble and simple
The easiest of fare
Toast and Tea

When you need a little comfort
Uncertain where to turn for it
Toast and Tea

When you are down
When you are blue
Toast and Tea

You serve it to others
Yet it also serves you
Toast and Tea

It is homey and pure
A delight for sure
Toast and Tea

The simplest of pleasures
One of life's little treasures
Toast and Tea

Brew a pot and let it steep
Brown a slice and savor deep
Toast and Tea

Accept the beauty of this little gift
Let it slow you and feel your mind shift
Toast and Tea

Seasonal Joys

Autumn:
Crunchy leaves
Pumpkins on porches
Crisp air
Warm browns, reds, yellows and oranges
Sunlight that changes and beautifully streams through sparse branches
Layering warmth
Wearing a coat for the first time this season
The last flowers of summer
A surprisingly warm day in the midst of cooling down
Feeling sunlight on your skin from your perch in the rocking chair
Annual traditions
Spicy flavors and tastes of the season
Drawing in as the days grow dark earlier
Gathering around bowls of soup, crusty bread, and candlelit tables
Celebrating thankfulness
A beautiful leaf or a perfect acorn picked up on an afternoon walk around the neighborhood
Time to put on the flannel sheets
All the apple and pumpkin recipes
Embracing the routine of everyday life and figuring out what works
Planning ahead and dreaming of Christmas
Pie
Plaids, sweaters, and fuzzy socks
Completion of a season of productivity, watching creation enter a season of rest

Winter:

Rosy cheeks
Mittens
Cocoa in favorite pottery mugs
Hidden work happening beneath the surface
A season of rest and slowing
The way sunlight streams through the front windows like no other time of year
Bluer sky and crisper air
Simple beauties of evergreen clippings, pinecones, dried oranges, and cranberries
Baking treasured and handed-down recipes
Honoring traditions
Sitting by the fire
A lazy afternoon reading a book
Music that feels like a familiar friend
Opportunities to give and serve
Lights abounding
Wonder, delight, and magic in watching children enjoy the season
A brisk walk
Hands wrapped around a cup of tea
Trying a new soup recipe
Lotion on chapped or dry hands
Adding an extra quilt to the bed
A hot shower
Putting clothes in the dryer and then getting dressed while they are still hot
Holly berries, plaid bows, the spicy scent of evergreen,
the yeasty scent of rising cinnamon rolls

Hot Chocolate
BAR

Spring:

That first warm day which prompts a deep breath of expectation at what is coming
New life
Tender green shoots poking their heads above the surface of the dirt
Optimism of cleaning out the garden and trying again
Blooming trees
Birds chirping in the mornings
The many shades of green
A season of remembering what God has done
The first day you can wear flip flops again
Butterflies finding their way as they flutter about the yard
A season of hope and new beginnings
Finishing up another school year
Picnics, salads, and eating on the porch
Daylight stretching out
Expectation and anticipation of growth
Life emerging from seemingly dead branches, proving that the
hidden work of winter is not wasted but restorative
Finding a bird's nest
That first yellow forsythia bloom
Going daffodil and strawberry picking
Still needing a light blanket to sit on the porch
Getting outside more
Propping open doors and sliding open windows to air out the house
Celebrating new life

Summer:

Wedges of cold, juicy watermelon dripping juice from chins
Sunflowers from the farmer's market
Road trips, cutting wildflowers on the side of the road, and a more relaxed schedule
Popsicles, salads, and ice cream to cool off after a hot day
Dipping toes in the ocean, pool, and creek
Picnics, hamburgers, corn on the cob, enamelware, and vintage coolers
Sundresses, quilts laid out under a shady tree, and a slow afternoon
stretching before you with nothing particular that needs to be done
Camping out in the backyard, reading by flashlight on the porch
Glowsticks and fireworks
S'mores and summer camp
Sunsets at the boat landing
Fan gently whirring to stir the air and keep the bugs moving
Watching fireflies dance across the way
Picking blueberries from the backyard to freeze, eat, and share
A summer thunderstorm
Smelling a neighbor grilling out while walking the dog
Freshly mown grass
Less routine commitments, more margin and flexibility
Going to a movie and wearing a light sweater for the cool blast of air conditioning
Adventuring and trying something new
Listening to the water
Lingering evenings as the light stays visible longer
Drawing a line through completed projects
Eating outside as often as possible

Soup and Grilled Cheese

Our rained-out (again) camping trip opened the door to some friends sharing their mountain cabin. Oh, what a time we had! The damp, chilly air invited all sorts of cozy activities, and we lived it up to the full.

Living in the South, we don't get much cool weather, so wearing coats is considered a treat. One cold day, the simplest of lunches was on my menu plan: slices of store-bought sourdough bread gently spread with soft butter, laid on a hot griddle, and cooked with squares of cheese oozing between the slices.

Cut in triangles or squares, this simple food is a magical delight! Popping open the lid of a can of soup makes the perfect pairing.

Golden. Crispy. Melty. Gooey. My children were so appreciative of the warm and cozy meal, and I admit that I enjoyed it tremendously as well.

Stepping away from the regular demands of life has a way of increasing my appreciation and appetite. Appetite for things that comfort, that inspire, and that give my soul a deep breath of peace and stillness.

How can a simple sandwich be such a gift? Perhaps the easiest answer is that it is familiar and homey – a reminder that someone cares about us.

Perhaps we think of our childhood with little circle slices of banana eaten with a toothpick for fun, and squares of toasted bread and cheese on the plastic Tupperware plate. Perhaps we remember that it is one of the first meals we learned to fully execute on our own, adding grilled cheese to our repertoire of cereal and toast!

I remember a day, as an adult, when I met a co-worker for a picnic lunch. She made grilled cheese and poured soup from a thermos, and I thought it was the most delightful picnic menu! We sat on a quilt, and I still remember that meal twenty years later.

There are now hundreds of variations on this creation, but let's admit it – the basics of just bread and cheese are simple enough to satisfy most of us. Go turn on the skillet, pull out the bread, and get ready to savor the comfort and simplicity of a grilled cheese sandwich.

Homemade Ice Cream

Blender whirring eggs and milk together.

Mom stirring the custard on the stove.

Silver canister chilling in the fridge.

Dad brings out the wooden cylinder and sets it on the back stoop.

Ice and salt are made ready.

Pretty soon I hear the motor running and see the wet spot on the cement stairs.

Brownies bake.

Ice tumbles in between the canister and wooden slats.

Salt is sprinkled in.

Ice and salt repeat.

The motor stops – Dad checks the churn.

The frosty silver canister is whisked into the freezer to await dessert.

Brownies are sliced and served into Corelle bowls.

Cold, sweet custard is spooned over the top.

Spoons serve up this summery treat and tongues dance with delight.

Time stands still on a slow, lingering summer evening.

Bread

Humble ingredients
Simple and pure
Homey and comforting
A healing cure

Mixing and kneading and
Time now to rest
Scent of dough rising is
Simply the best

Anticipation of
What is to come
Can cheer the spirits of
One who is glum

It says someone loves you
Somebody cares
It is an offering
You want to share

Bread must go into an
Oven that's hot
To rise, steam, and bake
In braid, loaf, or knot

Fresh bread from the oven
A lovely treat
With butter or jam
A delight to eat

Deliver a loaf to
A friend or two
A gift from yourself
To someone who's blue

Just as your dough has to
Go through a lot
Pressing and squeezing and
So very hot

You will endure things that
Challenge you too
On the other side
You'll find it is true

That beauty and change are
Not born through fear
But rather through struggle
New growth appears

Bread baking requires
A little more time
The waiting is worth it
Tastes so divine

When you are tempted to
Rush and just quit
Remember the lesson
To slow down a bit

The waiting brings beauty
And it brings hope
A peace for your journey
To help you cope

Bread is much more than just
Nourishing fare
It's art and a lesson
For you to share

It shows in your kindness
And in your face
It shows in your friendship
And in your grace

It points to our Savior
Who gave His all
How we treat others is
Part of the call

A simple loaf of warm,
Delicious bread
Can be a message of
His love instead

So bake bread! Eat it up!
Savor the gift!
Make it and share it
Give someone a lift

Flour and water, some
Salt and some oil
Put on a kettle of
Water to boil

Have a tea party and
Put on a smile
Make a new memory
Sit for a while

When you have finished and
Put things away
Bask in the glow and the
Gift of today

Set cares aside for an
Hour or two
You'll never regret the
Time spent it's true

So bake bread! Eat it up!
Savor the gift!
Make it and share it
Give someone a lift

Each day, the Lord loves us
He shows how He cares
May our lives be an offering
We are eager to share

WELCOME
FRIENDS

A Special Invitation

"Well, Come In!"

On Tuesday night, April 7, 1982, I was lying in a bed with a yellow and white headboard and a pastel rainbow bedspread pulled up over my five-year-old self. I don't remember all the details, but what I do know is that I realized there was something that I wanted to settle. As tears filled my eyes and my mom sat on the edge of my bed, in whatever way I could at age five, I remember realizing that if I died, I would not go to heaven, and I wanted to change that. My mom talked and prayed with me, and that night changed everything. That night in a corner room of a rental house in Kansas, my relationship with Christ began.

I knew that something was hindering me from having the assurance of heaven that I was looking for. And that something is sin. Sin is what separates us from God, and we can never cover up or clean out our sins on our own. Yet in His infinite love, God has provided a way for our separation to be broken! He sent His Son Jesus to Earth, to die on a cross and pay the price for my sin and for yours. Jesus obeyed and did exactly that, and then three days later, He was raised to life again. His death and resurrection have paved the way for us to be restored to a right relationship with God, and to spend eternity wrapped in the warmth of His love!

This same assurance I was looking for is available to you as well. It takes only the faith of a child to respond to Him and acknowledge that sin is separating you from Him, that you are asking forgiveness and receiving His free gift of salvation. That's it.

As a child, we would travel to see some extended family in Indiana. One visit brought an epic greeting that has remained a saying in our family through the decades. We went to a senior apartment complex to visit my dad's Aunt Doll, a very petite lady with fluffy white hair and a joyful heart. She opened her door and declared, "Well, come in!" She added a little accent for hominess, and it was a genuine and delighted welcome.

This is the friendship that Jesus extends to you, dear one. He is knocking at the door of your heart and waiting for the kind of welcome that my Aunt Doll gave: "Well, come in!" In Revelation 3:20 we read, "Behold, I stand at the door and knock. If anyone hears my voice and opens the door, I will come in to him and eat with him, and he with me." This invitation feels so cozy!

Just picture this – He is standing at the door of your heart, knocking. Will you answer the door? What will the welcome be? As seen in the verse above, He wants a relationship with you. Inviting someone into our homes is inviting them into a sacred space. This is where we let our hair down, put on our stretchy pants, and eat chips and salsa for dinner. He wants to be invited into this sacred space – where it is just the two of you sharing a cozy meal. I like to picture two chairs pulled up in front of the fireplace, my feet tucked up underneath my legs, a cup of something warm in my hands, a candle lit – and in the sweetness of this, He is in the other chair. He wants to be with *me*, with *you*.

Just as Aunt Doll greeted our family, so He is ready to welcome anyone who comes to Him. Just as I have shared my story, I would love to hear yours – please email me at therustyrobin@gmail.com if you have questions about this or want to share your story.

Romans 15:7, *"Therefore welcome one another as Christ has welcomed you, for the glory of God."*

Acknowledgements

Giving Thanks

So many times in the process of this project, I almost gave up. Wondering if it was something I needed to finish or if it was just to enjoy the process of writing. In the end, I can only say what I always say when someone asks how I get the things done that I do. Number one: there are things I don't do. Number two, and more important: God provides. I've long said that the only way to know He wants it to be done is that it gets finished and He provides the time and resources needed to accomplish it. Even nearing the end of this project, I wondered if it would ever be finished. Yet, here I am writing the acknowledgements page. A true gift indeed. Thank You, Jesus.

Am I the only one who really enjoys reading acknowledgements in the backs of books? I've noticed some common names and threads over the years of digesting these pages and while the names may not personally mean something to you - they definitely mean something to me and this book would not be complete without each one.

Special thanks to Katie Williams, my editor par excellence, who came alongside me in the most generous and kind ways during the levels of edits with this book. This project is exponentially more professional and clean thanks to her suggestions, kindness and genuine care for me as a writer and this project. You have gone above and beyond, my friend. Long live the Oxford comma, Katie, thank you for preserving it here and for your gift to me and these words. Visit her at www.storyborncreative.com!

I'm so grateful for my Writing with Grace friends who have helped me to recognize and embrace the fact that I like to write cozy things. That is my voice and it is not less than any other writer, just different. You have given me the push and permission to be the writer I am and to even call myself a writer.

Giving Thanks

Genuine thanks to so many who appreciate and enjoy cozy things along with me.

I'm grateful to Bella Grace magazine for publishing several of my pieces over the years which grew a confidence in me that my writing was worth reading and that writing about cozy things was beautiful.

Mom, thank you for loving this collection so much. Your encouragement bolstered me when I was wavering on finishing this. Not only that, but you love cozy too and are so good at encouraging things I love.

My heart is full of gratitude to my family who appreciates and values cozy as well. Thank you for all the evenings snuggled on the couch watching movies, many tea parties and picnics and trips to Camp Cozy. Home is my favorite place and that is a testimony to each of you accepting me for who I am and giving me the freedom to be myself in our home. I hope you feel the same comfort you have extended to me. Thank you for encouraging me to write and cheering me on in the completing of this book.

Finally but also with the fullest heart - a deep and profound thanks to my Heavenly Father for allowing me to serve You in this way. My heart is that these words will be a comfort, a place of peace but also ultimately a nudge towards You. I offer this up to be used however You see fit. It has been a sacrifice of praise but also a delight and joy to pour myself out in these pages. Thanks be to God.

About the Author

Monica Wilkinson

Born in Missouri. Raised in Colorado. Currently in the coastal lowcountry of South Carolina.

I remember a summer on our culdesac in Colorado Springs. My friend, Angie, and I would plan out little VBS events for our siblings and neighbors including lessons, crafts and activities. Later in a basement apartment when I had more than enough time and wasn't sure how to fill it, I started filling notebooks with Bible Study ideas. I guess you could say these are the beginnings of my writing journey.

There are no degrees to tell you about, no credentials to list here. I'm simply a writer. I feel lost without a pen and paper to jot down things I'm thinking about and have been known to write on receipts, junk mail and anything else I can find. Writing is one of the ways I process the world and life around me. This offering is a collection of these moments of processing.

When I'm not writing, I also love photography, studying the Bible, reading, spending a cozy evening at home and making everyday moments special.

My husband, David, and I have three teenagers and a snuggly beagle.

Most importantly I am a daughter of the Most High. This is the only credential that really matters, He is the reason and source of anything good that comes out of my life. To God be the glory, great things He has done.

SLOW
Slow Lane
THE BEAUTIFUL ART OF SLOWING DOWN
MONICA WILKINSON

Slow Lane

Slow Lane

Breathe deep.

Let it out slowly.

Imagine you are on a bustling highway in a sleek, speedy car. Traffic is cutting in and out all around you as everyone is in a hurry for some reason or another.

Now imagine trading that in for the family car on a winding, scenic country road. There are trees lining one side and a beautiful open meadow on the other.

Our culture wraps up a jam-packed schedule and frantic pace and sets it on a silver platter, offering it like a trophy to anyone who wants it.

But I propose we take that glittery package back and exchange it for a less traveled road, one that celebrates and enjoys the precious, everyday moments of life.

Let's move into the *slow lane* and unwrap the gifts the Giver of Life bestows on us every day.

Won't you join me in slowing? Step into these pages which are a unique combination of personal journal, Bible study, practical ideas and visual inspiration for slowing down. Start looking for the everyday beauty in slow!

Available on Amazon.

Beauty Maker
THE MINISTRY OF GOD-GIVEN BEAUTY
MONICA WILKINSON

Beauty Maker

Beauty Maker

Step into this interactive handbook that combines journal prompts, projects and Bible study as you pursue the one true Beauty Maker and learn how He has equipped you to create and enjoy beauty as well.

Who is a beauty maker? Aside from learning about God and beauty in the Bible, consider how you bring beauty to both your own life and the lives of those around you. Every time you give a hug, snip a flower, enjoy a sunset or listen to music you are a beauty maker. When you lighten a load, serve a meal, care for your home and more - you are cultivating beauty.

If you have an appreciation of beauty - this book is for you! If you desire to have an appreciation for beauty - this book is for you! Either way, these pages will guide you through thinking about God, who created beauty, and how we use the gifts He has invested in our own lives.

Each chapter includes journal prompts for you to process what you've learned and ideas for both cultivating and enjoying beauty. Hands-on projects are included which will allow you to create beauty for yourself or to share with someone else. Consider how beauty can be a blessing and how we can honor God by enjoying His beauty!

Available on Amazon.

In Loving Memory
Dan Odell
1952-2018

Thank you,
dear readers!